Wings
over sands

by

John Nixon

For Ross and Jenny Blanchard

First published in Great Britain 2012

First Edition 2012
ISBN 978-0-957-10219-4

Graphic Design by Russell Holden
www.pixeltweaks.co.uk

Printed and bound in the UK by Elanders

Published by

Introduction

As a very young boy, it was Cark airfield which first captured my imagination and sparked a lifelong interest in the history of Britain's wartime air bases.

I suppose that it was somewhat ironic that my first prison service posting should be to HMP Gartree in Leicestershire; the site had been home to Royal Air Force Market Harborough during the war years (a heavy bomber conversion unit). Some of the airfield buildings and traces of runway were still to be seen and I spent a great deal of my spare time poking around them.

In 1988 however, I transferred to HMP Haverigg in Cumbria. I was overjoyed to find myself working in what was broadly speaking, an air base which had simply been enclosed by a fence. Over the 28 years I served there, I slowly gained a broad knowledge of the site's history. I was also able to establish an annual reunion for veterans, many of whom became good friends.

In late 2009, I published my history of RAF Millom (No 2 Bombing and

Gunnery School, 2 Observer Advanced Flying Unit and their mountain rescue activities). I have since thought that this was putting the cart before the horse somewhat, as I always intended my first attempt at writing to be a history of RAF Cark. However, the story of the Flookburgh airfield site has involved a great deal more research than anticipated and it has proven to be more complex and diverse than I first imagined, since it traces its origins back to the days of the Great War.

As I delved ever deeper, I discovered the existence of RAF Grange-Over-Sands, an Equipment Officers' Training School based in the requisitioned Grand Hotel at Grange, which also trained Batmen (not superheroes, officers' servants) and ladies of the Women's Auxiliary Air force in practical mess management. My research has been very rewarding and has produced many photographs and quite a few surprises!

All facts stated with certainty were directly obtained from the Operational Records Books (ORB) – a daily diary of RAF Cark and RAF Grange-over-Sands – or quoted from service men and women who were witness to events and incidents at the time.

The Author

John Nixon was born in Ulverston in 1953 and attended High Newton Primary School. Later, on leaving Cartmel Church of England School in 1968, he made his living in many varied ways until he joined Her Majesty's Prison Service in 1974. After 32 years service, he is now retired and a self-employed writer. John is also the author of "Oh Mother it's a Lovely Place", a history of RAF Millom and their mountain rescue activities.

for more information about John and his books please see his website
www.johnnixonauthor.co.uk

Contents

CHAPTER 1

Winder Moor, Flookburgh
The Giant Airship Factory That Never Was

Whilst recently browsing a television listings magazine one evening, I saw advertised on the History channel, a programme about an extraordinary reunion which had taken place in Japan. It was in fact a reunion for kamikaze pilots. I was extremely curious and imagined something which involved a spiritualist and candles! It transpired however, that these were men who, having been prepared for their destiny, would have history and events pass them by as unrequired. Such was the case with regard to Flookburgh's airship factory, however rather than it being a 'none story', it is in fact a fascinating one and a story which is not widely known, even within the geographical location of its origin.

I am deeply indebted to Mr David Parkin who very generously provided me with the information necessary to illustrate this opening chapter on the primary usage of the Cark airfield site.

Flookburgh is a small village located several miles west of Grange-over-Sands, adjoining Cark in the northern shore of Morecambe Bay. Prior to the First World War, the West Lancashire Territorials had a rifle range just west of Humphrey Head. In 1911 a halt was built for their use at Wraysholme Crossing on the Furness Railway line. The platforms on the up and down side of the line were of timber construction and cost £120 to complete.

In 1916 Vickers Ltd decided that they needed a larger airship construction facility than the one they operated on Walney Island, Barrow-in-Furness. They chose the flat area called Winder Moss, south of Flookburgh for the site. By 1916 much larger airships were entering service and Walney lacked a sufficiently large landing area to accommodate them. It may well have been the Barrow site's vulnerability to attack, which also prompted the move to a larger and safer location.

On the 29th January 1915, a German U-Boat surfaced off the coast and fired several shots into the shipyard and the airship construction area of Vickers, causing alarm, but fortunately not inflicting much damage. It must have been a consideration at the time that the extreme sandbanks and relatively shallow waters of Morecambe Bay, gave protection from such an attack on the Flookburgh site.

The firm in charge of construction was to be A J Main and Company, with Sir William Arral as the contractor. Arral's, a well-known and major engineering firm, were responsible for among many other things, the construction of the Forth Railway Bridge. More importantly, they had just finished the erection of an airship construction shed for Beardmores at Inchannon on the Clyde.

This project was completed at the end of September 1916 and may well indicate an early November starting date for the Flookburgh facility. By late November, work was well under way. The minutes of the Furness Directors' meetings refer to eighteen to twenty wagons a day arriving at Cark Station in connection with the work at the airship site. Further, they estimate that some 45,000 tons of material would be required for the project. Proposals for a railway siding, at a cost of £750 were discussed and shortly afterwards Vickers requested the construction of a branch line from Wraysholme Crossing to the site, at an estimated cost of £1,400. The Furness Railway Traffic and Works Committee, on the 29th November 1916, authorised a siding for fifteen wagons. The branch line to the proposed airships buildings was also agreed and put in hand.

In December 1916, a piling survey was undertaken to determine the state of the ground. A signal box controlling the junction opened on the 26th March 1917, with a trailing connection to the up line and crossover road. An interesting feature of this was that when the box closed, the signals controlling the junction were operated from the crossing keepers frame.

Wraysholme Crossing present day looking towards the Winder Moor site

The railway branch line was completed by May 1917, running through to what is today known as Ravenstown, with branches to the sheds and Hydrogen Plant. A surviving ground plan of the proposed site shows that the sheds were to be located south of Willow Lane, with ancillary buildings to the north and south of the lane. A large hydrogen gas plant, capable of producing 50,000 cubic feet of hydrogen per hour, was to be located east of the hangers along with two large gas holders. The site, if it had been completed would have been enormous, being of double width and measuring some 900 feet long by 300 feet wide and 150 feet high, a less than subtle alteration to the local sky line! Surviving photographs of the shed build for Beardmores on the Clyde give a good indication as to what the finished structuring would look like, although it was much shorter and of single width. It is a matter of record that the estimated cost of the Flookburgh shed alone was £106,190.

The whole Flookburgh project was cancelled by September 1917, but only after the huge sum of £792,000 had been expended. It is highly likely that work never did get past the preparation of the foundations. Various reasons were given at the time to explain the cancellation, including trouble with the aforementioned foundations and the fact that the shed would have consumed a vast 7,000 tons of steel for the framework and cladding, plus the two very large wind screens. At this stage of WWI, steel was in short supply and it is entirely possible priority was given to the manufacture of the new motorised tanks making their presence felt on the front line. Some ninety three years after the event, we shall never know.

For those who love facts and figures!

The first payment recorded from Vickers on the 'Flookburgh Siding' account was £1,000 on 17th March 1917. Following payments were: £5,000 on 6th April 1917, £1,826 on 15th May 1917, £3,300 on 31st May 1917, £4,750 on 9th July 1917, £6,752 on 31st July 1917, £4,652 on 31st August 1917, £8,920 on 24th September 1917, £4,532 on 6th November 1917, £12,771 on 7th January 1918, £25,000 on 9th July 1918 and £10,000 on 20th August 1919.

According to records, salaries are first mentioned in May 1917. At £26 for a month, they increase to £33.16 in June and £83.10 in November. They then fell to £50 in February 1918 and remained at that figure until their last appearance in August 1919.

A cashier took up post in May 1917. Their weekly expenditure went from an initial £141 to £197 during that month, to between £200 and £220 for June. In July weekly expenditure was from £260 to £360. Weekly expenditure varied wildly from £280 in August to £250 during September, £250 to £370 in October, £240 to £290 in November, falling sharply during December. By January 1918 cashiers weekly expenditure was between £75 and £160 and by April had decreased from £50 to £80, a level at which it remained generally until the last payment by the cashier was noted on the 7th November 1919.

On a much lighter note and quoting from 'The Tee Square' magazine of Christmas 1917, the charity raising Journal of Vickers Armstrong's Drawing Office, Barrow-in-Furness, the contributed article was entitled 'The Drawing Office Abc' and was written by W.B. Under the letter 'V' was written the following:

V stands for Vickers
And you can never tell.
They might find you a job
At their place in H*** (Flookburgh)

One can imagine that this ditty very well described the chaotic state of affairs at Flookburgh in 1916 and 1917. However, by the time the article was published the whole project had been scrapped!

Postscript: The only part of the project to survive is the village of Ravenstown, formerly called Flookburgh Model Aero Village, and Flookburgh West, which was constructed to house the workforce. Vickers completed some of the accommodation to house workers from Barrow. Ravenstown was originally planned to be three times the size of the estate we see today, the contractors being J Parnall and Sons of Rugby and Rainey Brothers. For those who wish to delve further, Barrow Records Office holds an extensive file of documents relating to these houses. They cost about £400 each to build and were of dubious quality initially, with many problems related to water ingress.

The village was completed in 1918 and all the streets are named after WWI Battles: Jutland Avenue, Somme Avenue and Marne Avenue etc. In 1919 the site was turned over to the Disposal Board of the Ministry of Munitions by the Admiralty as totally un-saleable. Then in 1921, it was handed over to the Office of Works. Very little information is available as to what happened to the site between the Wars apart from the fact that all sidings and the site's signal box were removed on the 31st August 1922.

A time of peace with portents of further conflict

In the early afternoon of the 30th June 1936, the giant German airship 'Hindenburg' passed over Flookburgh on its way to America. The Barrow news for the 4th July 1936 reported, "The German airship the Hindenburg paid a surprise visit on Tuesday afternoon when it passed over the village at 2 o'clock. Flying very low, the low steady drone of its engines heralded its approach and indicated to the villagers that some unusual visitant was in the vicinity. The residents were quickly out of doors and in the street to watch its progress. Flying low and steady, an excellent view was obtained. Details of the hull and name were easily discernable; with a bright sun shining on its silvery grey body, it presented a wonderful sight."

A wonderful sight indeed! However, due to the rise of the Nazi party in Germany, there was some concern about the possibility that 'Hindenburg' was in fact spying and the Member of Parliament for Barrow, Sir Jonah Walker Smith, asked questions in the House on the subject. Previously, on May 22nd, the same Zeppelin had passed over the bay between Barrow and Morecambe. It seems highly probable that the 'Hindenburg' was carrying out some sort of reconnaissance of the industry on the Furness peninsula and also wherever its flight path took it.

The Hindenburg

Could it also be that the Germans, perhaps knowing of Flookburgh's proposed airship works, were taking a sneaky look to see if any sort of aircraft industry was being resurrected at the site? With the clouds of war once more gathering on the horizon, the Zeppelin was about to pass into history, to be pushed aside by more formidable aerial weaponry, which was to give the slumbering Flookburgh site a new life and purpose once more.

CHAPTER 2

1941
The Construction of RAF Cark Begins

Work on RAF Cark began in the early summer of 1941 and was undertaken by contractors John Lang and Son, who at the same time were building nearby RAF Walney. Cark was constructed under the jurisdiction of 9 Group Fighter Command (Speke Sector) and was built in the wake of the German blitz on northern industry and the considerable damage inflicted upon Barrow-in-Furness.

As a fighter aircraft station the airfield layout was broadly typical of design for that period. Three runways, two of 1,100 yards and one of 1,300 yards were laid in a triangular pattern with the usual perimeter track running round them to allow access to taxiing aircraft.

RAF Cark 1942
Image courtesy of RAF
Hendon Museum archive

Along the eastern side of the airfield were six dispersal pens, each of which was designed to house two fighter aircraft. On the other side of the site a single Bellman hanger was erected for any major aircraft servicing requirements. At a later date, hanger space was supplemented by the erection of fourteen Blister hangers. Their construction was to provide cover for minor servicing work, but not least of all to protect the aircraft from the salty corrosive winds which routinely buffet the area around Morecambe Bay.

Twelve of these Blister type hangers actually formed the technical area which was in the north- west corner of the aerodrome. Situated so close to the dispersed living accommodation, an aircraftsman could almost literately fall out of bed and into his spanners!

As part of airfield defence, pill boxes, gun posts and a Battle HQ Bunker were sited at strategic points across the airfield. Also sited were a large number of air raid shelters, many of which survive to the present day, several still in good condition.

Of interest is the block house type pill box which is situated on the shore at the very end of Moor Lane. This gun post offered an extensive view over Morecambe Bay and was intended to provide a forward defence in the event of an enemy landing upon that stretch of shoreline.

Airfield Pillbox

Air raid shelter southern edge of airfield

Block house gun post at end of Moor Lane

Blast shelter adjacent to workshops

Whilst all the Blister type hangers are long gone from the aerodrome, the Bellman hanger survives as a listed building to the present day. Indeed, many of the sites original buildings also survive to be hosts to various industries and in some cases act as stables and stores. Survival of the airfield's Control Tower is most definitely assured as it is now a domestic dwelling.

Control Tower - present day with watch office in foreground

Let Flying Commence!

By the new year of 1942, the German aerial bombardment of the area had subsided, due largely to the pressure on the Luftwaffe brought about by Hitler's Russian campaign. Thus it was decided that a fighter station was no longer needed at Cark and the airfield was re-allocated to Training Command, opening on the 17th March 1942 as a Staff Pilot Training Unit, an entirely new organisation.

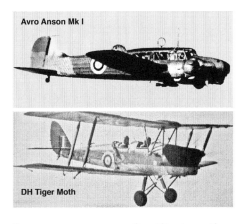

Avro Anson Mk I

DH Tiger Moth

The unit was formed under 25 Group. Its purpose was to familiarise pilots with the type of flying being done at Air Observer Schools before they were posted to these in an instructional capacity. A good number of these pilots, though not all, had undergone initial training overseas.

Throughout its life the unit operated the twin engine and extremely reliable Avro Anson aircraft, a machine used broadly across the whole spectrum of Training Command. Additionally, a Tiger Moth was used by the station for communication purposes.

Also arriving on the 17th March was 'R' Flight of No 1 Anti-Aircraft Cooperation Unit who had, for some six months, been a 'lodger' unit at RAF Millom pending the completion of RAF Cark. 'F' Flight No 6 Anti- Aircraft

Artillery Camp

Cooperation Unit also transferred to the station from RAF Ringway, better known to us today as Manchester Airport.

These units were to be based at Cark to carry out aerial target towing duties over Morecambe Bay. This facilitated the training of anti-aircraft gunners of the Royal Artillery, whose equipment and men were already beginning to arrive at the station.

Westland Lysander

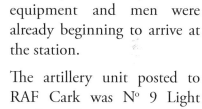

Hawker Henley

BP Defiant

The artillery unit posted to RAF Cark was Nº 9 Light Artillery Unit operating their 40mm Bofors guns. They were based in a largely tented site south of the airfield and in the area now occupied by a caravan park.

The AACU's were operating Westland Lysanders, Hawker Henleys and Boulton Paul Defiants. Their task was to tow a target, which resembled a large wind sock, behind their aircraft whilst trainee anti-aircraft gunners took pot shots at it under the directions of their Commanding Officer. Not a job for those of a nervous disposition I'm sure. However, station records do not mention any 'friendly fire' mishaps resulting from this particular facet of the training at Cark and this I consider highly commendable!

Also arriving on the 12th March was Sqn Ldr J.C. Gibb who would stay in post as Station Commander for the duration of the unit's life. Sqn Ldr Gibb's Miles Magister aircraft was a common sight in the local skies as he routinely performed aerobatics over the sands. A larger-than-life character, Sqn Ldr Gibb is remembered by all who knew him a very 'hands on' leader who would turn out regularly for search and rescue duties and participate fully in the station's social activities. Not least of all due to his unique approach to command, the unit at Cark was known locally as "GPAF" or "Gibb's Private Air Force"!

By the 27th March some thirty aircraft were in post, of which ten were Ansons for Staff Pilot training duties. It had been decided that the unit would attempt to maintain a minimum pupil population of forty, with the first course set to commence as soon as possible. On the 15th April however, the station's ORB (Operational Record Book) records, "Owing to the non-arrival of technical equipment, No 1 course cannot commence instruction. Commencement of course deferred until the 30th April 1942".

This was indeed to be the date of Cark's very first training course and compromised of two Officer Grades and nine Sergeant Pilots, all of whom were to pass out successfully with an average air time of 55 hours 25 minutes per pupil. Sadly no photograph of this course has come to light.

Over 1st and 2nd May ORB records the arrival of F/O Ross as station Medical Officer and six nursing orderlies to staff the unit's Sick Quarters which it was proposed, should be established at Mill House, Flookburgh. To this end, an inspection visit was paid to the property by Wing Commander Gibb (now promoted) and Sgt Kent of Grange-over-Sands police.

On the 12th May at 11:00 hours the airfield received notification that an aircraft had crashed on nearby Hampsfell. The Senior Medical Officer and two nursing orderlies left the station by ambulance to search the area, but very quickly established that it was a false alarm and were recalled by 12:10 hours.

Three days later on the 15th May ORB records, "10:30 hours, defence conference held in station HQ, medical subjects discussed: (1) establishment of first aid posts in station (2) duties and operation of stretcher bearers (3) collection and evacuation of casualties during air raids or land attacks on this station".

It was decided that first aid posts should be established at station Headquarters (SHQ) and N°1 Anti-Aircraft Cooperation Unit. Also, those parties of stretcher bearers should operate from them. Additionally, the first aid posts should be staffed by medical orderlies and the Medical Inspection Room

W/Cdr Gibb (on left) & Sqr/ Ldr Skingsley with Miles Magister aircraft

should be used as a casualty clearing station – evacuation of casualties would be to Conishead Military Hospital, Ulverston. To supplement space a further station Sick Quarters site was suggested: the property on Flookburgh Square owned by Mr. Avis and a visit was arranged to facilitate this.

By the 2nd June no WAAF contingent had yet arrived to take up post at Cark, though all their accommodation was completed and ready to receive them. Until such time as these postings arrived, ORB records that, "This accommodation be allocated to airmen as the provision of living accommodation for them was still on going".

Up until this point, RAF Millom had been acting as 'parent' station to RAF Cark. From an accounting point of view however, this changed on 1st July. Cark become self-accounting with Flight Lieutenant D.M. Millar posted in as Senior Accounting Officer.

On the 15th July RAF Cark experienced the first of two accidents which were to happen within three days of each other when Anson DG785 and Anson DG787 collided whilst landing almost one on top of the other! Fortunately there were no casualties from this mishap. However, both aircraft were so severely damaged as to be considered un-repairable.

Far more fortunate was the pilot of Hurricane AG338 of 46 Maintenance Unit (MU) Lossiemouth making a safe forced landing at Cark after the aircraft developed problems with the Merlin engine's coolant system.

Training courses now fully underway

Nº 2 Course
Standing L to R – Sgts Edwards, Isfield, Dickenson.
Seated L to R – Sgt Miller, P/O Speler, P/O Johnstone, P/O Oddie, W/O Davison

Nº 3 Course
Standing L to R – Lloyd, Smith, Taylor, Witt, Kaye
Seated L to R – Dixon, Jupp*, MacDonald, W/O Powell, Robertson, Page, Bainbridge

*P/O T.Jupp subsequently lost his life flying from RAF Millom. See book one 'Oh Mother, it's a lovely place'

Nº 4 Course
Standing L to R – Sgts Bishop, Cumby, Gibson, Williams, Griffiths, Dorman, Baker, Longhurst, Bratt, McReady, Fairweather, Blakemore.
Seated L to R – W/O McLennan, P/O Sutherland, P/O Robb, P/O Jeffrey, P/O Timms, P/O Hoslin, P/O Hodgson , Sgt Kirkwood

However, two days later on the 17th July, the station suffered its first major tragedy. Anson R9640, out on exercise, struck high ground on the Isle of Man resulting in the death of her three man crew: Sgt Gibson and Sgt Dorman of Nº 4 course and wireless operator Sgt Parsons, a sobering incident for the station.

On the 9th August Cark's emergency crews were called upon once again to await the arrival of a Tomahawk fighter aircraft which was to make a forced landing with engine problems. The approach was successful but the aircraft crashed on touchdown, resulting in severe damage to the airframe, but leaving the pilot uninjured.

Across the country, Training Units were rapidly phasing out the Blackburn Botha aircraft due to its lack of power and its lethal tendency to develop engine failure during takeoff and in flight. Designed as a torpedo bomber, it never saw service and was swiftly reassigned to Training Command where it gained a

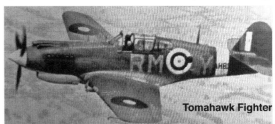

Tomahawk Fighter

dire reputation. So it was then that no one raised an eyebrow as Botha L6243 made a forced landing at Cark on 25th August with a port engine failure, to be followed the very next day by yet another Botha when ATA Pilot Officer May made a belly landing due to starboard engine seizure! Happily both pilots were uninjured.

Blackburn Botha

On the 27th August the station MO proceeded to Low Holker Club where airmen from the station were billeted and upon inspection found conditions to be entirely satisfactory. Meanwhile back at the airfield, a very jolly time was being had by all participants as they were introduced to the delights of the Army Mobile Gas Chamber Training Unit! Station ORB records, "2 minutes spent exposed to gas with mask, then 2 minutes exposed to gas without masks". I am sure the Army enjoyed it immensely!

Nº 6 Course
L to R – Sgts Payne, Shearer, Bramer, P/O Bower, P/O Hannagh, F/O Clarke, P/O Cox, Sgt Close, W/O Harrington, Sgts Arrand, Chadd, Parker, Punter, Collier, Birch, Bryson.

Nº 7 Course
Standing – Sgts Brown, Cornwallis, Royle, Burkes, Francis, Rhude, Archer, Hole, Wilson, Houghton, Shutt.
Seated middle – Sgt Anthony, P/O Lindsey, P/O Zatdel, P/O Wallis, Sgt Cooper.
Seated front – Sgts Austin, King, Mallinson, Long, Lockhart, Shapley, Pool

Alongside the Avro Anson, the Westland Lysander remained a remarkably reliable and safe workhorse whilst employed at training establishments around the country. At 10:50 hours on the 18th September however, one of Cark's Lysander's suffered a complete engine failure upon take off and crashed almost directly opposite the station's flight office. It is recorded that the aircraft was a complete and total wreck but that its pilot, Sgt Jordan 1375082 escaped with little more than minor abrasions to his hands and legs. Rescue of Sgt Jordan took place rapidly due to the close proximity of the flight offices and though fire services quickly attended, no fire was ignited in the accident.

As with many outlying stations, RAF Cark often provided an emergency haven for aircraft in distress, however on occasion, such landings could result in mishap. On the 21st September ORB records, "Hurricane aircraft crashes on its landing approach. Pilot F/O Methan of RAF Milfield, Northumberland found 20 yards to the rear of his aircraft having died from skull fracture and multiple injuries."

The 15th October brought news of a further tragedy when word arrived by phone from the Yorkshire constabulary that a Mustang fighter aircraft which had been missing for 24 hours had been located, crashed at Daw Haw near

North American Mustang

Settle. The aircraft was found to be broken up over a fairly large area and the body of its pilot, P/O Hainey (an American) still remained at the site of the impact. The police duly mounted a guard on the accident and Cark's ambulance, station Medical Officer and an assembled team made their way there immediately. They were met at the scene by F/O Davies who was from the pilot's parent station of RAF Ouston. After identification Cark's team removed the body of P/O Hainey and arranged transport for him back to RAF Ouston.

It can be difficult to establish the time and facts surrounding incidents and accidents which occurred some 70 years ago, but very often versions of events persist. We know for a fact that the Gypsy Moth biplane of Cark's Anti-Aircraft Cooperation Unit made a forced landing on what is now Grange Golf Course on 28th October. In doing so it overturned very close to where Grange gasworks used to be situated. We also know that its pilot P/O Brooks and his passenger Sgt Johnson, escaped unharmed from this unfortunate state of affairs. The version of this story I have been told suggests that the two intrepid aviators in question may have been conducting an impromptu aerobatic performance for the ladies of the WAAF at the Equipment Officer Training School, which was based in The Grand Hotel when misfortune struck – oh dear!

"I THINK YOU CUT THAT LAST LOOP A BIT FINE, SKIP"

Some five days later at 13:00 hours on 2nd November, Cark's station Sick Quarters received notification that an aircraft had been seen to crash at Scaleber Force near Settle in Yorkshire. The station MO with a team of volunteers left immediately by Humber ambulance and very quickly located the crash site. The aircraft was an Airocobra and was totally destroyed, its pilot being found dead some 400 yards from the wreck having bailed out of the plane too low for his parachute to open. He was second Lt Cecil I Rhodes aged 23 years of 92 Fighter Squadron USAAF.

Bell Aero Cobra

For some weeks, discussion had been taking place with regard to the disbandment of the SPTU at Cark and its transfer to a different location, but leaving the AAC Units in place as lodger units. All this was resolved on the 14th November when it was officially decided that the SPTU should remain at Cark after all and be re-designated No 1 SPTU.

1943 Onwards and upwards!

With the Unit's future assured, 1942 ended without any serious mishaps and Christmas was celebrated in good cheer. The New Year began in satisfactory manner and by early April 1943 unit staff numbers stood at:

Airmen and Airwomen............. RAF 524 and WAAF 210
SPTU Pilots .... 60 and 30 WO/AG Under training
SPTU Aircraft on strength....... 28 Ansons, 1 Magister, 1 Martinet and 1 Master

Furthermore course No 11 had just ended and a new signals instruction block was nearing completion ready for an intake of pupils due to arrive later in the month.

The month had begun on an optimistic note and on the 10th April, Grange-over- Sands held their 'Wings for Victory' parade in fine style attended by WC/DR Gibb. A contingent compromised of 50 RAF and 50 WAAF marched through the town and later attended a dance at Grange's Victoria Hall. Staff Pilot Course No 12 which commenced on the 19th April consisted of 30 pilots, all of whom had just completed training at Advanced Flying Units.

Is it Cork, Cask or Cark? hic!

A shadow was cast over the station two days later, when on the 21st of the month, Anson N4953 broke up in mid air and crashed into Main Street, Warton, Lancs. Her pilot, Sgt Pittendrigh, a New Zealander (who was flying solo) was killed instantly. Incredibly ORB records, "No civilian casualties resulting from the incident and Sgt Pittendrigh was buried in Cark churchyard with full military honours."

Nº 12 Course

Back L to R – Sgts Conning, Draycott, Bunting, Green, Woods, Armstrong, Wisby, Bannea, Waigh, Harvey, Galley, Mackay.
Middle L to R – Sgts Bowen. Gallacher, Wilkinson, Wright M.T., Wright G.E., Burton, Dawson, Day, Koninburgh, Burns, Hurley, Mortimer.
Front L to R – Sgts Ferguson, Fisher, P/O Bramer, F/LT Lowe, F/O Anderson, P/O Barlow, Sgt Spotswoode

Nº 13 Course

Back L to R – Sgts Shaw, Lawrence, Creelman, Wilson, Wiggin, Ansell, Taylor, Martins,
Middle L to R – Sgts Shaw HL Simpson, Briggs, Wilkinson, Scott, Folliott, Phipp, Frazer, Atkins, Bullock. Hackworth, Bates, Mould.
Front L to R – Sgts Froud, Hobbs, P/O Holtby, Campbell, P/O Smith, S/Ldr Gearing. F/LF Lowe, P/O Cumming, P/O Ross,
P/O Browne, Sgt Swinton.

April ended with the expected intake of fifteen wireless operators. The course was to be taken in the unit's wireless training block which was now in operation.

Ground based wireless training

It would appear that the station grew as much of its vegetable produce as possible. The ORB on the 6th May records the establishment of a "gardening night", instituted for unit food production to be held every Thursday night between 18:00 hours and 20:30 hours. This was another example of W/ Cdr Gibb's dynamism in his command of the station by engaging with the national "dig for victory" initiative of the time.

High winds were still a feature of the weather in early May, as on the 7th May ORB records: the fact that Anson R3375 suffered extreme damage to its tail section whilst taxiing in a gale. Fortunately no-one was injured and its removal for repair would cause no shortfall in training as further aircraft had been steadily arriving at Cark over the previous two weeks. With the arrival of a further three Anson's the next day the station now had thirty-eight on strength and serviceable, plus four more under repair/scrapping.

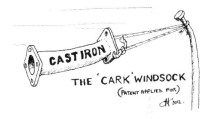
CAST IRON
THE 'CARK' WINDSOCK
(PATENT APPLIED FOR)

Whilst gas was never used as a front-line weapon during World War II, the horrors of its use during the Great War were still very strong in the minds of the government and the military. So much so, that upon the outbreak of the Second World War, gas masks were issued to the armed forces and civilians alike.

Whilst communities, schools and factories etc were holding gas mask drills, military personnel were being made more acutely aware of the lethal potential of an enemy gas attack. They were being trained accordingly, even to the extent of the use of a very potent and dangerous mustard gas during live exercises.

On the 14th May Cark's ORB recorded, "A demonstration involving the use of live mustard gas was given under group auspices. At 09:30 hours two chemical mines were blown up on the South East perimeter of the station and the area, approximately 300 yd, was then decontaminated and marked off with gas warning signs."

Two days later at 15:15 hours on the 16th May, the local Gas Identification Officer carried out a test on the detonation area and found it safe to walk on. However, such was the potency of the gas that the site was deemed unfit for occupation for a further 48 hours.

The month of May drew to a close with the arrival of fifty WAAFs, some Balloon Operators and some Flight Mechanics under training. All were to receive six months training at Cark as Flight Mechanics (engines and airframes). Additionally ORB recorded, "For the first time in the history of the unit, the task chart was completed, and the 2,084 flying hours agreed upon was exceeded by 30 hours; the total night hours for the month being 734 hours and 30 minutes. 18 members of No 11 course passed out as Captains of Aircraft – this course suffered 4 wastages; one killed, two withdrawn from training and one posted to a Pupil Advanced Flying Unit for further training. Those passed out as captains of Aircraft were of good average standard. Also, 21 members of No 12 course passed out as Captains of Aircraft on 31st May 1943. A flying accident occurred last night 30th May 1943; no personnel were injured. The accident was due to an error of judgement on the part of the pupil pilot who overshot the plane path when landing in a dead calm on returning from a navigational detail."

The month of June 1943 brought much improved weather and balmy temperatures. On the 28th June, the fourth anniversary of the birth of the WAAF was celebrated by the ladies of 1 SPTU, the event being a resounding success. Following on the 30th was a station sports day which was well attended and prizes were presented by the station Commander's wife, Mrs. Gibb.

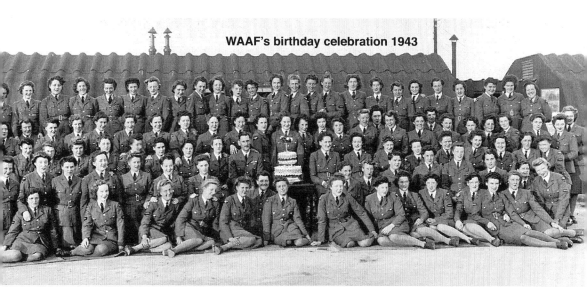

WAAF's birthday celebration 1943

July brought the very same weather conditions as its predecessor, conducive to reaching target training hours for both day and night flying. Insofar as the daily life of the station is recorded, neither problems nor incidents occurred. One is left with the impression of a well commanded and indeed happy unit, with a vibrant social life both on station and in its interaction with the local community.

With the coming of August, the situation was to change somewhat, not least of all from a meteorological point of view. The weather suffered with unpredictable variations in conditions, often suddenly and on at least one occasion, violently and dangerously. On the 3rd August 1943 at commencement of night exercise, Anson N5123 swung off the runway due to an unpredictable cross wind and crashed causing extensive damage to the airframe, but leaving its pilot P/O Ledger uninjured.

By this time the following Courses had passed out successfully...

Nº 14 Course
Back L to R – Sgts Gooder, Gray, Veevers, Taylor N.E. Roberts, Martin, Gillespie, Findlay, White, Cock.
Middle L to R – Sgts Ware, Taylor L.W, Lund, Cowley, Kent, Hardwick, Couling, Smith, Forbes, Hill, Coggins, Clarke, Benson.
Front L to R – Sgt Robarts, P/O Ferris, P/O Goodrum, F/O Walters, F/O Anderson, P/O Robertson
P/O Cumberbirch, Sgt Hay

Nº 15 Course
Back L to R – Sgts Thorpe, Healy, Burdett, Kennedy, Weller, Sedin, Toppin, Bennett, Hick, Tebbutt
Middle L to R – Sgts Ling, Speed, Hislop, Tonks, Russell, Deane, Couley, Cooper, Tennyson, Laing, Williams.
Front L to R – Sgts Hick, Holdsworth, Emmerson, F/O Smith, F/L Lowe, F/O Wise, Sgts Benn, Hickilligan, Bromley, Staple

Nº 16 Course

Back L to R – Sgts Brownlee, Hicar ? Knipson, Ablett, Williams, Pendson, Spurr, Holt
Middle L to R – Woodward, Clarke, Lalmide? Saundes, Horman, Schinkel, Strangeways, Jonhstone, White
Front L to R – Livingstone, Tonkins, ? Waterhouse, Walters, Hierchant? Tremider, Van-boolen, Mitchell

Nº 17 Course

Row 1 – Sgts Furnish, Cooke, McGhee, Phillips, *unknown*, Cochrane, Cowie, Speed. Horne
Row 2 – Sgts Wickwar, Roberts, *unknown*, Sawyers, Mathers, Coles, Hillman, Strang, Finan, Hutton
Row 3 – Humphreys, Williams, Maclean, Smeltzea, *unknown*, Ashwell, Ledger, Collinson, Cranham
Row 4 – Darby, Old, Wastnage, Caswell, Brooks Twyford, Connolly

Meanwhile at another very busy training airfield several miles away up the west coast, RAF Millom (N°2 OAFU) was steadily building a reputation as a very capable Mountain Rescue unit. This reputation was to result in the team being co-founder member of today's RAF Mountain Rescue service.

On the 18ᵗʰ August 1943, they received what was to be their first major challenge. They were called upon to locate and attend the crash site of an Avro Anson, lost during a navigational exercise whilst flying from its parent unit RAF Dumfries (N°10 OAFU). Millom's team had no idea however, of the extent to which they would be stretched until word arrived early the next day that a further three aircraft were missing, presumed lost in the Lake District mountains.

Official records are frank in their admission that meteorological forecasts for the 24 hour period covering the 8ᵗʰ and 9ᵗʰ August proved inaccurate to say the very least. Conditions encountered by those who flew that night have been described as terrifying. Pilots and crews had been briefed to expect light to moderate west to south westerly winds, at times reduced visibility and some precipitation. What they encountered by contrast, were tornado strength winds, hailstorms and lightning strikes, making navigation extremely difficult and a swift return to base a necessity.

Most aircraft landed safely. However, four victims of this freak weather event were located crashed upon the high ground of the Lake District when dawn broke the next day. The crash site of DJ275 of RAF Dumfries was found on Cam Spout, just below the summit of Scafell and it was clear that all had been killed instantly. They were (Pilot) Flight/Sergeant Kawalczyk, Sgt Chadwick, Sgt Pickering, Sgt Denson and Sgt Lawson.

A further search revealed Anson DJ229 of RAF Dumfries on Green Gable, N5053 also of RAF Dumfries on Great Dodd and Anson L5986 of RAF Babington at Carrock Beck Heskit, this aircraft crew all having survived the crash. One member of aircrew lost his life in the Great Dodd crash and a further two in the Green Gable incident. It was a disastrous night for the RAF and an exhausting one for their embryonic mountain rescue teams. It could however, have been much worse.

With a large number of aircraft now overflying the same high ground in the north-west, it must have been felt that some involvement by RAF Cark in a mountain/crash rescue capacity would be at some point inevitable. Whatever the reasoning behind it, on the 10ᵗʰ August, S/Ldr Skingsley (C/O Training), F/Lt Williams (Medical Officer) and F/Lt Ardron (Signals Officer) visited the crash site of DJ229 on Green Gable. Presumably they visited with a view to familiarising themselves with such terrain and formulating some sort of long-term logistical strategy with regard to search and rescue in this type of environment.

On the 22nd August however, the unit was itself to lose an aircraft closer to home, when Anson LT146 undershot on approach to the airfield and crashed into the sea just offshore. Despite the fact that this was during night flying detail, the pilot, W/Off Macadams was located and rescued uninjured.

The fact that Cark was readying itself for rescue duties is given further substance on the 30th August when ORB records, "The following personnel attended a crashed Oxford aircraft on a hilltop near Dent (Yorkshire). S/Ldr Skingsley (C/O Training), F/Lt Williams (Medical Officer) and F/Lt Ardron (Signals Officer)." Also of interest is a record entry on this day of arrival on the station of Officer in Command Technical Training, Air Marshall Sir A .Barrat, accompanied by Air Commodore Quinnell, Group Officer McLeod (WAAF), W/Off O.Hackforth-Jones

Airspeed Oxford

(WAAF), S/Ldr Holmes and St/Off Lambell (WAAF). All travelled on to the Short Sunderland flying boat factory at White Cross Bay Windermere, by road. And having concluded whatever business took place, returned to Cark and left by air the following day at 17:55 hours.

At close of proceedings on the 31st August 1943, ORB records, "Flying hours for the month of August were 1,454.20 (day) and 659.10 (night). Adverse weather at night resulted in night flying hours being below the target set for the month."

The month of September saw improved weather conditions and an increase in flying training. This included night navigational exercises which most

pilots found very tiring. With clearer conditions, the Bofors guns of the adjacent Anti-Aircraft Training Unit were merrily blasting away at their airborne targets as pilots and crew of the night flying details attempted to sleep. I am reliably informed that said pilots and crew found this very tiring too!

It was not at all unusual for aircraft to be dispersed out on the grass areas at Cark due to limited hanger space and a lack of suitable "hard standing" only rarely presented any problems as the airfield was generally quite well drained. This was not to be the case on the 8th October when following a sustained rainstorm it was found that Anson LT429 had become "bogged down" in the wet ground overnight.

At 10:30 hours, the decision was taken to attempt to tow the aircraft back to the perimeter track by use of one of the station's tractors and a team gathered around the Anson to push as the tractor gently pulled. The degree to which the aircraft's wheels had become embedded in the soft ground had been severely underestimated however. Both undercarriage units collapsed leaving LT429 in the undignified position of 'belly down' in the muddy ground. On the 15th October, a similar fate befell Anson EG686 prompting much debate about the advisability of parking aircraft on open ground during the wet months of autumn and winter.

The weather for the month of October was summed up thus in the station's ORB, "Flying hours for the month were 1,135 hours Day and 594 hours Night. Adverse weather conditions experienced during the month held up flying training considerably. The most noticeable feature of the month's weather was consistently poor visibility, due to smoke from the individual areas of Lancashire. There was appreciable rain or drizzle at some time during the day on 13 occasions; during the rest of the month the weather has been mainly cloudy".

It was as a result of this dismal and dangerous weather, that on the 30th October; no less than eleven of Cark's Ansons were forced to abort their daytime navigational exercises and divert to make forced landings at other stations. The following nine aircraft landed safely at RAF Valley, Anglesey:

Anson NG235	Anson DG931
Anson EG640	Anson EG682
Anson DJ182	Anson LT427
Anson EG637	Anson LT359
Anson MG22	Anson's LT427 and EG605 diverted and landed safely at RAF Jurby, Isle of Man.

November was to bring much improved weather conditions, though with at least one exception when Anson R9693 was forced to divert to RAF Golden Grove due to adverse conditions. Whilst carrying out a forced landing there, the aircraft crashed due to a failure of its port undercarriage unit. Fortunately, her crew escaped with little injury.

The November weather was described in the station's ORB thus, "We have seen a departure from the general idea of 'dull November' with clear skies and a lot of ground frost. Mock suns observed during the daytime and very clear sightings of the Aurora Borealis on several nights. Most interesting atmospheric phenomenon!"

AN IMPRECISE SCIENCE!

Like the curate's egg, the weather at Cark was good in parts!

Flying hours recorded at the close of November were 889 daytime and 795 night making a total of 1,684.

On the 1st December, the status of Cark's Anti-Aircraft Cooperation flights, were officially recognised when they were formed into 650 Squadron AACU. Gunnery courses continued to pass through the Artillery Camp with Miles Martinet aircraft being used almost exclusively for aerial target towing duties.

Cark's ORB carries two notable entries for the 20th December. The first concerns Anson EG700 out on a night navigational exercise from the station. The aircraft developed engine problems out over the Irish Sea, but was able to make a safe forced landing at RAF Valley.

Miles Martinet

The second entry records the notification by land line of a catastrophic aircraft crash near Coniston. A team led by the station's Medical Officer left Cark to attend the scene of the accident. The crash site was easily located due to the devastation caused to the area. A Barracuda aircraft of 747 Squadron was on a night navigation exercise from Royal Naval Air Station Inskipp. It had crashed close to High Arnside House, killing all three crew members and creating a large crater in the landscape.

The destruction surrounding the crash was due to the fact that the aircraft was carrying a live torpedo at the time. Fragmentation was such that small pieces turn up from time to time even to the present day. Those who perished in the crash were Sub L/T G.F. Hopewell, W.H.R. Young and D.Buttery, RNVR. Whatever the cause

Fairey Barracuda

of the accident, the operation to deal with the aftermath would prove to be one of the most challenging and grisly tasks undertaken by Recovery Units locally during the war years.

Thankfully the rest of the month appears to have passed with little more in the way of notable incidents and Christmas was celebrated in good cheer by all ranks! Total flying hours for December 1943 were 1,149. As the new year began, little seems to have hindered the Staff Pilot training programme. No 28 course arrived on station along with a course of twelve W/Ops who were to undertake instruction both in the air and in the station's signal training block; its purpose built classrooms completed and in full use.

It was upon returning from a night navigational exercise in less than ideal weather, with poor visibility on the night of the 19th January, that Anson EG605 came to grief in strange circumstances. Knowing that they were close to home and spotting what they believed were the welcoming lights of RAF Cark, they began their landing approach, only to realise at the very last moment that they were in fact trying to land on Lancaster Railway Station! Realising that they were on completely the wrong track, (couldn't resist that one) they hastily aborted their attempt and tried their luck - more successfully this time - on the other side of Morecambe Bay. I am reliably informed that a further incident had occurred previously which involved Carnforth Station.

By now twenty nine staff pilot courses had passed through RAF Cark and training of WAAFs and wireless operators continued to run smoothly, whilst the gunners of the artillery units continued to blast away noisily at their airborne targets...

Nº 18 Course
Back L to R – Sgts Marshall, Buckler, Mehew, Story, Manning, Gayler, Wright, Williamson, Smith, K.M. Johnson.
Middle L to R – Sgts Davis, Forder, Streeter, Hancy, Sheehan, Syme, Cathcart, Rowlands, Sowerbutts
Front L to R – Sgts Smith, W.S., Bell, Porter, Lea, *unknown, unknown*, Sgts Percival, Stoker, Dix, Brockett

Nº 19 Course
Back L to R – Sgt Hoagg, McKenzie, McGeachy, Hill, Miles, Knight, Gibson, Gilliland, Kirby, Rose.
Middle L to R – Sgts Boston, Taylor, Patton, Mills, Coxon, Newman, Allen, Celerier, Shaw, Lord, Carter
Front L to R – Sgts Whitely, Cooper, Woodrow-Smith, P/O Kirkbride, F/O Wise, P/O Staples, Sgts Stubbington, Murray, Howarth

Nº 20 Course
Back L to R – Sgts Fudge, Proudfoot, Pagram, Reed, McMaster, Redburn, Hill, Stephens, Thompson, Shage
Middle L to R – Sgts Flemons, Gilmore, Brown, Stevenson, Godleman, Troth, Moore, Muddell, Dring, Eastman
Front L to R – Sgts Davis, Lintott, Anderson, Grant, Taylor, F/O Walters, Sgts Poole, Bruce, Pavey, Hide

Nº 21 Course
Back L to R – Sgts Dudderidge, McLeod, Blake, Isaacs, Stokes, Pilling, Barnie, Fewtrell, Wilson
Middle L to R – Sgts Flynn, Falconer, Morrison, Lamb, Dunbar, Phillips, Lucas, Thorpe, Jewer, McDonald
Front L to R – Sgts Palmer, Petitt, Grant-Taylor, F/S Hearle, P/O Gray, F/O Wise (staff), P/O Maguire, W/O Kaiser,
Sgts Kirkpatrick, Brooks

Nº 22 Course
Back L to R – Sgts Clarke, Lindsay, Neillands, Downes, Battishall, Jeffries, Knutton, Birks, Crver
Middle L to R – Sgts Samuels, Robb, Stubbs, Roberts, Gillette, Garnham, Bell, Ryden, Buckle, Keeler
Front L to R – Sgts McGolrick, Moore, Little, P/O Binns-Ward, F/O LNSmith (staff), F/O Hole, P/O Montrose, Sgts Colton, Taylor, Figures

Nº 23 Course
Back L to R – Sgts Prout, Bell, Sargent, Milner, Harding, Cole, Banks, Dyson
Front L to R – F/Sgt Fox, F/Sgt Dunn, W/O Rose, P/O Jennings, P/O Walters (staff), P/O Gurr F/Sgt Mali, F/Sgt Bushfield, Sgt Darnell

Nº 24 Course
Back L to R – Sgts Eckersley, Ford, Roddy, Robinson, Goldsworth, Rosochacki, Page, Pickles
Front L to R – Sgts Nowak, Peacock, P/O Bailey, F/O Walters (staff), F/O Cochrane, P/O Martindale, F/Sgt Macnamara

Nº 25 Course
Standing L to R – Sgts Gruszezvk, Usejsky, Winterbottom, Park, Tomlinson
Seated L to R – Sgt Slimon, F/Sgt Remington, P/O Jackson, *unknown*, F/Sgt Nedrychowski, Sgts Burton, Douglas

Nº 26 Course

Back L to R – Sgt Evans, F/S Clarke, F/S Bennett, Sgt Standing, Sgt Burton, F/S Craske, F/S Bartrum, F/S Freeman, F/S Helmer, F/S Bain
Middle L to R – Sgts Jack, Hayes, Jacobs, Biffen, Bryant, PF Jones, Usherwood, Tosney, A.C.Castle
Front L to R – Sgts Bridgman, I.Jones, A.E.Castle, Coppard, F/O L.N.Smith (staff) F/S Wilson, F/S Trendall, F/S Cleaver, F/S McConnell

Nº 27 Course

Back L to R – Sgts Rainer, Bayntonn-Power, Plumb, Cameron, Rimmer, Holden, Richards, Dee, Hunt
Middle L to R – Sgts Fail, Old, Matthews, Woods, Birt, Mills, Long, Mcgarthy, Lewis, Johnstone, Fortune
Front L to R – Boxall, O'Connor, Marston, Lansdell, Beck, Mooney, Davies, Freeman, Allingham

Nº 28 Course

Back L to R – Sgts Summers, Sund, Wilkin, Clement, McLeod, Pitchers, Evans, Sayfritz, Perry
Middle L to R – Sgts Nell, Anderson, Reid, Dupuis, Bottomley, Harvey, Gooch, Delaney
Front L to R – Sgts Brooks, West, P/O Boyd, P/O Norman, *unknown*, P/O Rabzak, P/O Lawrie, Sgts Pitt, Leech

Nº 29 Course

Back L to R – Sgts Orgill, Prentice, Wilson, Griffiths, Moore, Birch, Mason Porter, Ashton, Henley
Middle L to R – F/Sgt Ryan, Sgts Thomas, Keppie, Cundy, Mayhew, Grant, Singleton Wyatt, Rees, Wheeler, Watson
Front L to R – F/Sgt Quinn, P/O Steinman, F/O Stewart, F/O Turnbull, W/O Walters, S/Ldr Grace, P/O Page, F/O Gaudett, W/O Robinson, F/Sgt Crotty

February brought poor weather once again. This may have contributed to the damage sustained by Anson EG686 when it made an otherwise safe forced landing at Cark due to engine problems on the night of 7th February. Then misfortune struck the station once more, when on 18th February, Anson W1651 crashed on the perimeter of the airfield due to loss of power on take-off. No injuries to her crew are recorded and as my late dear pal P/O David Waters used to say, "Any landing you walk away from is a good one!"

By the 20th February, station logs speak of snow, sleet and hail driven by strong winds. This may well be the reason why on this date Anson MG433 was forced to divert to Llandwrog on Anglesey after leaving Cark that night, for a navigational exercise. Whatever the reason was for the diversion, news arrived at Cark by landline that MG433 had crashed on its landing approach to RAF Llandwrog killing the pilot and leaving three crew members seriously injured. Such an incident always cast a dark shadow over the happy station, but as one who served there at the time told me "The War didn't stop for grief and the job went on".

On the 23rd February, an Anson on exercise from Cark crashed into the fields just between Birkby Hall and Cartmel. The crew escaped without injury and as the crash conveniently occurred at 12:00 hours they were taken back to Cark in time for lunch and subsequent refreshment in the station mess! The cause of the crash, I believe, was engine failure. It is to be remembered that whilst the Armstrong Siddeley Cheetah radial engines fitted to the Avro Anson had a reliability record which was second to none, by this stage of the War much had been asked of them in poor conditions, even given meticulous servicing on a regular basis.

Given the weather conditions throughout the month, flying hours combined totalled 1,939. This must have included some uncomfortable trips for pilots and crews.

March 1944 began in a tragic manner for Cark. During a night navigational exercise, two of its Ansons were involved in a fatal mid-air collision out over the Irish Sea. They were Anson EG231 and EG592, both on the first leg of their night exercise, outbound in the direction of the Isle of Man; a loss of both aircraft and eight crew members, I have been unable to establish crew names. It must be remembered that none of the radar and safety technology which exists on aircraft today was part of aerial safety or navigation at this time and that even keen eyesight and unflagging vigilance might not be sufficient to ensure the safety of aircraft and crew. With the many airfields of Training Command overflying the same areas, close encounters and near misses were common. I have been told first-hand of being passed so close at night by another Anson that turbulence from the propellers of the passing aircraft could be felt. It is fortunate in the extreme then, that whilst mid-air collisions did happen, they were not a more common occurrence.

An added hazard whilst night flying or indeed flying during daylight, but in bad visibility, was the prevalent areas of very high ground to be overflown during exercises. Snaefell in the Isle of Man, the Welsh mountains and those of the Lake District and Southern Scotland all posed a threat to air traffic flying at an altitude of less than 4,000 ft.

It is fair to say at this stage in the development of aircraft instrumentation, that in the case of the altimeter inaccuracies were not uncommon, often resulting in fatalities. We shall never know if this instrument played a part in what occurred on the night of the 20th March, but it is possible.

As Cark awaited the return of their night flying exercises, all seemed well and routine until contact was lost with Anson EG686 somewhere over the Irish Sea, on its return to base. It was assumed initially that radio failure was the problem, but as time passed and all other aircraft returned safely, fears for the missing crew mounted. By next morning it was obvious that an accident had occurred as no other stations had taken EG686 as a diversion or forced landing.

Aircraft were dispatched to search land and sea over the eastern section of the previous night's exercise and this included the western fells of the Lake District.

By late morning the wreckage of EG686 was located on the Coniston fells above the tarn of Levers Water, on the flanks of Swirl How and RAF Millom's now well experienced and established Mountain Rescue team were called upon to attend the crash site. When they arrived, it was clear that no rescue was possible as all on board had perished upon impact with the mountainside. On board EG686 were Sgt Butler, Sgt Younger and Sgt Snelling. It seems likely that realising that they had overshot, not only Cark but also the coast, they turned back on a north-westerly heading to take them out to sea, only to become trapped in the Coniston Fells.

Images of wreckage from EG686

1. Undercarriage unit
   (Author 1972)
2. Undercarriage
3. Engine cylinder
4. Propeller
   (unknown group circa 1970s)
5. Valve rocker cover, spark plug leads & fuel filter
6. Wing wreckage (Jane Tuck)
7. Engine
   (Jane Tuck & Russell Holden)
8. U/C winding mechanism

Solway aviation museum

Of interest at the close of March 1944, is the station's recorded personnel strength:

RAF Officers	82 includes 30 Staff Pilots under training
Airmen	531
WAAF Officers	4
Airwomen	215
Aircraft	42 Avro Anson
Aircraft	1 Magister

Resulting in a total of 832 various ranks in post, it does not include personnel in post on the adjacent artillery camp. That represents quite a social impact upon a small community like Flookburgh. It must however, have sent cockle, shrimp and beer sales through the roof!

April brought with it poor weather and a number of mishaps, the 6th April ORB records, "Anson LT738 of 10 AGS Barrow-in-Furness landed at this unit with damage to rudder, tail plane, elevator and wing, caused by mid-air collision." The 13th April records, "Cark Anson EF863 'belly' landed at Royal Air Force Millom, extensive damage to aircraft." The 15th April records, "Cark Anson MG227 forced landed at Ronaldsway, Isle of Man with

wireless failure, damaged tail on take-off due to having hit an obstruction on runway, starboard undercarriage fractured." Finally, on the 24th April ORB

records a visit from Sq/Ldr Marsden who was visiting the station on behalf of the Air Ministry Accident Prevention Section. During his visit and just as it was about to take-off, Anson LT435 crashed into a ditch just off the runway and wrecked its undercarriage. I wonder if Sq/Ldr Marsden proffered any advice.

What a month April had been! The combined total of flying hours was much lower than normal at 1,555 and the station's ORB records, "Inclement weather held up courses considerably, resulting in two course extensions being requested."

An integral part of training at Cark involved bomb aiming and to this end the station maintained a bombing range just off shore near Silverdale where small practice bombs were dropped on a wooden target. Each bomb carried a powder charge which released a visible cloud upon detonation. This enabled range plotting staff to assess the accuracy of each drop and log the results.

Practice bomb heads from Silverdale range

This was not the only activity carried out from the station, as 650 Squadron's aircraft routinely towed practice targets for the anti-aircraft units based close to Heysham. Also based alongside the Light Artillery Units, were the heavy anti-aircraft guns at two other locations on that section of the coast to protect Heysham docks from attack.

It was following a target towing flight for the Heysham artillery that on the morning of the 3rd May a Martinet of 650 Squadron made a forced landing on the beach at Humphrey Head. The beach in those days would've presented a large expanse of flat, fairly firm sand. It is now however, fast becoming salt marsh, with the only landings carried out successfully by geese!

Hawker Hurricane

Servicing Hurricane in Bellman hangar

It is worthy of note that the month of May also saw the arrival of the first of a number of Hurricane MK IV aircraft which were being flown in to carry out target towing alongside 650 Squadron's Martinets.

By the 16th May up to and including No 37 Staff Pilot's Course had been completed and the successful participants awaited their postings.

Nº 30 Course
Back L to R – Sgts Caan, Schlightinger, Smith, Reed, Morrell, Prior, Stockill, Karpinski, Stewart, Scovell, Stevenson
Middle L to R – Sgts Cox, Blanchard, Jorgensen, Prentice, Bull, More, Webster, Robinson, Parfitt, Jorden
Front L to R – Sgt Galletley, P/O Rose, P/O Holubowicz, F/O Sowerbutts, F/O Baxter, F/O Rook, P/O Radon, P/O Lech, F/Sgt Newcombe

Nº 31 Course
Back L to R – Sgts Hailwood, Knighton, Jachacz, Knight, Blant, Jorden, Quail, Parry, Brettell, Pearce
Middle L to R – Sgts Kidger, Haden, Chesher, Brackenborough, Cowell, Reilly, Price, Dodkin, Chapman Tuckey, Sullivan
Front L to R – Sgts Barker, Shelling, Cook, F/O Magness, F/O Smith (staff) F/L Kurowski, P/O Barlow, Sgts Bullock, Edwards, Rychlik

Nº 32 Course
Back L to R – Sgts Tickner, Derrick, Williamson, Bennett, Cherry, Szredski, Wood, Korris, Brooks, Davis
Middle L to R – F/Sgt McArthur, Sgts Rowbottom, Stackowiak, Juczyszyn, Romanowski, F/Sgt Cook, Sgts Polkowski, Odolewicz, F/Sgt Saville
Front L to R – Sgt Korny, P/O Dateson, P/O Brice, F/LT Grifllth, F/O Walters (Staff) F/LT Mauksell, F/O Milne, W/O Sercombe, F/Sgt Staton

Nº 33 Course
Back L to R
F/Sgt Harper, Sgts Morris, Drennan, Beaumont, Turnbull, Chapple, Mason, Smith, MW Whittaker, F/Sgt Ellis, Sgt McPherson, W/O Roberts
Middle L to R – Sgts Atherley, Ratcliffe, F/Sgt Pilgrim, Sgts Smith, L.Tait, Pheonix, Baldwin, W/O Dickenson, Sgts Letts, Bagwell
Front L to R – P/O Franke, P/O Leyland, F/O Barton, *unknown, unknown*, P/O Hollely, P/O Matthews F/O Jellinek, F/O Chamberlin, F/O Manning

Nº 34 Course

Back L to R – Sgts, Hoyle, Wakeman Wilson Fricker, Tanner, Green, Eades, Cox, Struthers F/St Burbury
Middle L to R – Sgts Wright, Roxbugh, F/Sgt kirkgard, Sgts Haigh, Phillips, Datman, Murray, Reltham, Frost, Ashbrooke
Front L to R – F/Os Richmond, Muncy, Dawson, Stenlake, Thomson, F/Sgt Squires, F/O Anderson, F/Os Salmon, Garne, Shaw, Matthews, Buggenhaut

Nº 35 Course

Back L to R – Sgts Hawkins, Banas, Sierkierkowsi, Gierszal, Aldridge, Fox, Randall, Bryant, Blake, Meysztowicz, Cylwik, Taylor
Middle L to R – Sgts Ellis, Murdock, Turner, Novis, Milner Spencer, Daniszewski, Zdeb, Zawadski, Gant, Danhoffer, Toombs
Front L to R – W/O Curtois, Travers, Bowder, Harvey, Boothby, Wise, Watson, Robertson, Massie, Eddy, Workman

The role of Staff Pilot at training establishments was an important one,
though to be chosen for this duty was often met with disappointment.
To reassure pilots that their contribution to the war was a very real one,
the station's magazine included the following article:

That course at Cark

Many people dislike intensely the idea of going on a course. It takes them away from
their familiar surroundings and friends; they have a natural feeling that they are better
employed where they are; they often firmly believe that the course is useless as far as
they are concerned; and in many cases they urgently desire to do something else. These
are the factors which operate in the minds of potential "course fodder" and, as we said
at the start, the result is that they just don't want to go.

Take, for instance, the Staff Pilot's Course at Cark. Here the last factor is probably
the most weighty. For every keen pilot, on leaving his (P) A.F.U., wants to do just one
thing – go on to an O.T.U. and get on ops. as soon as possible. Instead, he is told that
he has clicked for the Staff Pilot's Course at Cark, and as far as he can make out, all he
is to be trained for is merely to go into Flying Training Command and become a driver
for aircraft-loads of student air crew at (O) A.F.U's. Worse still, he ruminates, a large
part of the flying will be at night, probably in foul weather; it will be long dull "cross-
country's" or trips round the British Isles, not simple local stooges; and since the only
navigators he'll carry are u/t, they'll be frequently getting lost and he'll have to bring
them home. No future in all that. And to think that, instead, he might be shooting down
FW's. No wonder he is browned off when he hears he is to go to Cark.

And that is just why we want here to talk for a moment about the whole idea of the
Staff Pilot Training Unit.

First and foremost, we'll tell you definitely that no one who is sent to Cark is sent
because at some time or other he has made a boob, as a result of which a black mark
has promptly been put against him, and he is considered "only fit for Flying Training
Command duties". Quite the opposite, in fact.

A pilot detailed for this course is one whom the authorities think will get the fullest
value out of the training there and will perhaps be ultimately of even more use to the
Service and his country than if he went on to an operational squadron in the normal
way. He has in fact been selected, not detailed; it is an honour – though one that a first
he naturally doesn't appreciate.

And now we'll explain why this is so by telling you about the actual job the S.P.T.U.
pupils are being trained for.

They are to be Staff Pilot Captains at (O) A.F.U's. (A small percentage, however –
those who do best on the course – are picked for Staff Pilot duties at the Empire Air
Navigation School, a most interesting business, involving regular long-distance flights
to India, Canada, and so on.) Now the Staff Pilot's job at an (O) A.F.U. is not just a
boring chauffeur's job. It is work of the utmost value and responsibility. For the (O)
A.F.U. crew has, besides the Captain, only two u/t W/Op. and u/t Air Bomber as well.
To this lot, particularly the budding Navigators, the Captain has to be instructor as

well as pilot. He must assist them in every way he can and, above all, he is responsible for their safety. A u/t Navigator can, and does, boob – after all he's there to learn by practical experience – and when he does, the pilot has to get the aircraft back or, at any rate, safely down at some airfield. This means that he must be constantly checking in his own mind the courses given him – a very different thing from being able to turn to an experienced Navigator and say, "What's the course and where am I?" This in turn means that he must have considerable skill in mental D.R. and D.R. procedure; and must realise the Navigator's responsibilities and be able to help him by kind and timely criticism.

Added to all this, he must be capable of flying accurately by day and night, both visually and on instruments, in bad weather, over sea and over that small but very difficult and knobby country – the United Kingdom. He must, too – and this is vital, for he and his W/Op. are the only trained men in the aircraft – know all the safety aids, dingy drill etc.

And all this he is taught at Cark. Definitely he is not sent there because he has blotted his copybook. A Staff Pilot's job is probably one of the most difficult in the Air Force, for, unlike the operational pilot who has a full crew to help him, he has to help most of his crew, be able to fly accurately by himself and yet has all the normal worries of a crew captain.

Let's ask a final question? Whatever pilots may think about the course before they go to Cark, how do the feel after-wards? The answer is that they are practically unanimous in realising what a lot they have learnt, and how little they knew when they first came – including how much they thought they knew. They realise that before they joined they thought they had nothing to learn from the navigational point of view, when all the time they had been merely pushing an aeroplane through the sky instead of flying accurately as good pilots should. And, above all, they realise they have been given Confidence – confidence in themselves and in their own ability to do a difficult and valuable R.A.F. job successfully.

So take all this to heart, those of you who are going to Cark, and don't waste the first week or so of your course – as so many people do – in bemoaning your fate at being bunged in F.T.C., in indignant resentment at going back into ground school, in thinking you are fully trained and know it all, and in wondering vaguely about your future job and deciding that anyway it's valueless. Realise it is valuable; get cracking right away. Cark is there to get the best out of you. See that you get the best out of Cark.

N⁰ 36 Course

Back L to R – Sgts Reed, Albin, Cottage, Maybey, Langley, F/Sgt Greennell, Sgt Bomby, F/Sgt Goodil, Sgts Haxe, Bell
Middle L to R – F/O Taylor, Sgts Benford, Barr, Campbell, Miles, Jordan, Freeman, Brown, Agnew, Cooke
Front L to R – F/Os Ward, Park, Munro, F/Lt Graham, F/Lt Walters (staff) F/Lt Bartlett, F/Os Flenniken, Wilson, Louthood

N⁰ 37 Course

Back L to R – Sgts Waters, Maud, Leavens, Penonsek, Douglas, Green, Paterson, Misfeld, McLaughlan McCarthy, Whyham
Middle L to R – Sgts Bell, Gray, Baker, Pike, Asbridge, Conroy, O'regan, Verkon, Lofting, Phillips, Redfern, Young
Front L to R – Morrison, Hetherington, Isaac, Lindsay, Locke, F/O LNSmith (staff) Cottnam, Dyer, McKelvie, Leary, Levofski

The 18th May was marked by yet another accident for 650 Squadron when one of its Martinet aircraft crashed near Millom and burst into flames. It is fortunate that help was at hand in the form of an agricultural worker who was able to pull the pilot to safety. Due to the fire the aircraft was a total loss to the unit.

June was largely uneventful though with variable weather, resulting in slightly lower flying hours, the month's total being 1,556 with 564 of these flown as night details. At the many stations of training command where the Avro Anson was extensively used; the type had gained a solid reputation as a reliable and safe workhorse, earning the nickname "Faithful Annie".

However, by this stage of the war and after many hours flown it is possible that a number of these aircraft were suffering fatigue in certain areas. It is fair to say that one of the components which were to suffer the greatest stress was the aircrafts undercarriage, with landings at night and often in bad weather being made in a less than gentle way!

This may be at least part of the reason that on the 17th July, Ansons MG228 and DG574 both suffered undercarriage failures when returning from the same navigational exercise. Making belly landings on the airfield, both crews escaped uninjured with the two aircraft damaged, but repairable.

1944 photo of the celebration of WAAF 'birthday'

Only five days later on the 22nd July the station was to lose yet another aircraft when Anson LT359 crashed onto the fellside north of Millom near the village of Bootle. Her pilot F/O Lowe and his crew were rescued by RAF Millom's Mountain Rescue unit who were not only stationed nearby, but were also by this time, a very experienced team officially dedicated to the task of search and rescue.

July was brought to a close in a happier fashion by the station's sports day on the 30th. It is recorded that fine weather and a host of events were enjoyed by all ranks and that trophies and prizes were presented by the unit C/O's wife Mrs Gibb.

The 3rd August was marked by the arrival at Cark, of Vickers Wellington HF180, which I believe, had been detailed to deliver parts to the unit from its parent station of RAF Silloth. With their delivery completed and as the

Vickers Wellington

crew were taking off, the Wellington suffered a loss of power which resulted in a crash at the head of Cark's runway. No crew were injured in this incident and the aircraft having been badly damaged remained at Cark for some time before being eventually scrapped.

Meanwhile adjacent to their SPTU neighbours, 650 Squadron continued to fly daily drogue towing details for the Battery of Cark and also for those on the other side of Morecambe Bay in the coastal area of Heysham and Middleton Sands. It was also part of 650 Squadron's duties to provide drogue targets for air to air gunnery practice by trainees in other aircraft.

It was for the latter purpose, that at 15:05 hours on the 21st August, Flt/Sgt Harris left Cark and flew out to the firing range at Middleton Sands in their Martinet aircraft that day. On successful completion of the exercise the drogue target was released and the aircraft was seen to begin its return to RAF Cark flying low over the sands. It is thought that as Flt/Sgt Wilson banked to port in order to cross the bay; he flew toward the sun whilst doing so. This would most likely have resulted in a loss of perception of the height at which he was flying above the sands and his turn caused the aircrafts wingtip to hit the sand. The result was of course catastrophic, as this caused the aircraft to cartwheel and catch fire.

The two men were rescued by range personnel and taken to the Military Hospital in Morecambe (the Midland Hotel, taken over for that purpose in 1940), where sadly John Wilson died from his injuries two days later. SGT Harris however, quite remarkably made a full recovery and eventually returned to his duties with 650 Squadron. Flt/Sgt John Wilson was a New Zealander and had only been in post at Cark for a mere six days, he is buried in Torrisholme Cemetery, the only 'Kiwi' to lie there.

On the 22nd August the day after this tragedy Staff Pilot Course No44 arrived to begin training as the previous course began receiving their various postings. At 13:50 hours that afternoon a radio request was made by Halifax LW678 of RAF Burn for permission to make an emergency landing following engine problems. The landing was made at Cark without drama, however it was discovered that the propeller and entire reduction gear casing had broken away from her starboard outer engine. It was decided that repairs were beyond the resources of the unit and a servicing party were drafted in from No 4 Group to replace the written off engine and repair any damage inflicted to the surrounding airframe caused by the loss of the propeller.

Halifax Bomber

The weather report for August mentions generally fair conditions at the outset, then alternating days of cloudy then clear conditions with occasional rain. It is also of note that so much industry existed in Barrow-in-Furness and Liverpool at that time that it is recorded in the station's logs as decreasing visibility to such a degree that its pollution restricted flying at times. The hours for the month of August are recorded as 1,647 daytime and 872 night flying, a total of 2,519.

It can be taken as a mark of how bad the weather conditions were in September 1944, in that the Station Commander did not bother to record them! On the 1st September four Wellingtons made safe forced landings at Cark. The station's ORB records that the first seventeen days of the month made flying virtually impossible and that after a couple of better days the weather deteriorated once again, providing only four clear nights out of thirty.

October brought greatly reduced flying hours once again due to the very poor weather conditions which continued to prevail throughout the month. The station's ORB page for October only carries ten entries. These are mostly concerning visits by various officers from different stations and departments for the purpose of inspection or instruction.

One entry however stands out in stark contrast. On the 15th of the month, at fifteen minutes past midnight, Anson NK348 was approaching take-off speed travelling in a westerly direction when failure of its port engine occurred, resulting in a catastrophic swing from the runway in that direction.

The Anson now out of the pilots control struck a Nissan hut on the south west corner of the airfield. As a result of this, one of the huts occupants, Sgt Tatten of 650 Squadron was killed instantly, dying from what were described as "multiple injuries". All other personnel in the hut at the time escaped unharmed, as did the crew of NK348, from what was an unforeseeable and tragic accident.

The following courses were completed or ongoing...

Nº 38 Course

Back L to R – Sgts Holmes Bennett, Keeping, Fitzmaurice, Wunderlech, Holland, Goodall, P/O Miller, F/Sgt, Zawoony, Sgt Hughes, W/O Ostackowski

Middle L to R – F/Lt Hall, Sgts Clark, Clayton, Fittall, Davidson, Parsons,Hughes, F/Sgt Guerrier, Sgt Curtes, P/O Chmielrwski, Sgt Niewiardwski, F/O Richardson

Front L to R – F/Lt Robertson, P/O Fowler, F/O Watterson, P/O Eaton, F/O Baxter, F/Os Schoenhals, Morrisson, Carter, Milligan

Nº 39 Course

Back L to R – Sgt Grimer, Mayne, Shave, Brunskill, Richards, E.A. Richards, A.C. Sunderland, Miller, Russell, Foreman, Curran

Middle L to R – Sgts Rose, Ferrari, Dufty, Cherrington, Ickeringill, Towner, Tyrell, Claydon, Kelly, Formby, Forshaw

Front L to R – Scott, Johnson, McFayden, McDonald, W/O Brown, Summerbell, Vaughan, Lane, Bornip

Nº 40 Course

Back L to R – Sgt Lonnia, F/Sgt Wasiak, Sgt Doidge, Mather, Smith, F/Sgt White C/O Sgts Lyngh, Morton, Sadler, F/Sgt Madders
Middle L to R – Sgt Young, F/Sgt White TP Sgts Mason, Gumming, Laming, Lang, Flawn, Deboni, Newby F/Sgt Waters
Front L to R – Sgt Rzyskiewicz, W/O Piasecki, W/O Pietrzyk, F/O Liebiedzinski, *unknown, unknown*, P/O Sayer, F/Lt Davey, W/O Frankowski, F/Sgt Briggs

Nº 41 Course

Back L to R – Sgts Glenn, Bradley, Burgess, Searle, Tucker, Waterworth, McGillivray, Peacock, White, EJ McDonald, Bradford
Middle L to R – Sgts Aunger, McGarth, Richardson, Woodgate, McCallum, Terry, Gwartney, Nicholls, Brothwell
Front L to R – Sgts Graham, Daney, Cantor, Forbes, *unknown, unknown,* Sgts White, VO Dooley, Clarke, Mills

Nº 42 Course
Back L to R – Sgts Sparrow, McKinder, Baker, Kinninmont, Hilton, Needham, Bye, Ellison, Wright
Middle L to R – Sgts Levesque, Coleman, Shaw, Jeffery, Kautto, Thompson, Nicoll, Thiessen, Parkin, Russell, Murphy
Front L to R – Sgts McInnes, McBean, Hoare, Garrett, F/O Dean F/Sgt Archer, Sgts Thomas, Dorrington, Getliffe

Nº 43 Course
Back L to R – Sgts Reaume,Taylor H, Kielb, Michel, Adamek, Bosomworth, Roland, Barlow, Kosciuk, Keefe
Middle L to R – Sgts Drummond, Butler, Zaluska, Davis, George, Pamment, Rodriquez, Greenwood, Taylor, A Stack, J Witwicki, Jones
Front L to R – Sgts Beard, Stack, Cowper, Kaye, F/O Parkinson, F/Sgt Lorimer, Sgts Schroeder, Harrison, Findley

Nº 44 Course
Back L to R – F/Sgts Harrison, Tilley, Rothe, Sgt Lamont, F/Sgt Colgan, Sgt Pringle, F/Sgt Sanderson, Sgt Bridges, F/Os Pleak, Barnes
Middle L to R – F/Os Hall, Young, Shalliss, Sgts Stephen, Jolly, Wright, Wall, Anthony, Harris J Green
Front L to R – F/Sgt Seymour, Sgt Sweeting, F/Lt Longmuir, Sgt Doig, W/O Hall, Sgts Hayden, Harris, AJ Vanner, F/Sgt Steiner

Nº 45 Course
Back L to R – Sgt Stewart, F/Sgts Wilson, Berry, Sgts Bountiff, Wignall, F/Sgts Wood, Wild, Angus, Allan, Millington, Sgt Short
Middle L to R – F/Sgts Bunce, Ball, Griffin, Sgt Smith, F/Sgts Van der veken, Ward, Osborn, Sharp, Smith, Harrison, Hoatson
Front L to R – P/Os Dziewanowski, Juny, F/Os Beatley, Butcher, P/O Homes, F/Sgt Whitcoak, F/O Holland, P/O Walmsley, F/Sgt Macrae, P/O Cudzich

RAF Cark servicing wing

First group picture of permanent staff RAF Cark (officers and flying)

November 9th 1944 – a mystery of the sands

What follows is a story which has haunted, frustrated and confounded me since I had it first told to me by my father as a young boy. It is the story of an airman and his aircraft lost in the sands of the Leven Estuary on the above date that remain where they crashed to the present day.

The aircraft was on a test flight from 10 AGS Walney and was a Miles Martinet flown by W/Off Pyka, a Polish pilot who had been posted to Walney from 10 OAFU Dumfries. I have in my records three accounts of the incident and how it was dealt with and because two of them contradict each other I decided to devote some deep research into the matter with a view to establishing hard facts.

We must begin by looking at the three versions of this event as given to me, and then evaluate them using Admiralty Tidal Records and the station logs of RAF Walney and RAF Cark, which do provide a valuable time frame for the incident and its aftermath.

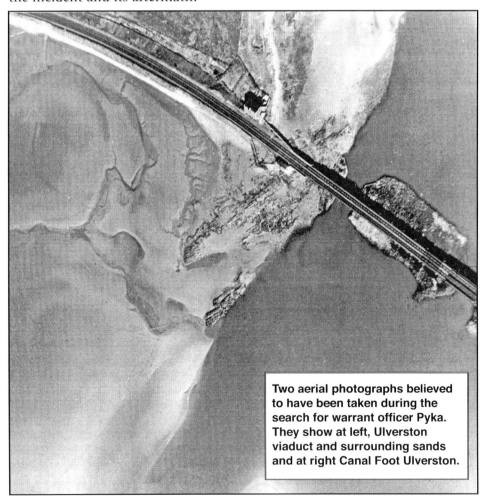

Two aerial photographs believed to have been taken during the search for warrant officer Pyka. They show at left, Ulverston viaduct and surrounding sands and at right Canal Foot Ulverston.

Account Nº 1

During the war years my father worked on the family farm at Greenhurst which is situated on the fellside above Cartmel. My grandparents Martha and Thomas Nixon also took in bed and breakfast guests to supplement their income. The farm proved a welcome retreat for many RAF staff from Cark and a very regular visitor who became a close family friend was W/Off Ralph Room. It was from Ralph that my father was told the story of the crash out on the sands and his version of events was as follows:

Word had been received late in the afternoon of the 9th November that an aircraft had been seen to crash offshore near Ulverston Railway viaduct. RAF Walney had received a distress call from one of its aircraft and suspected that the plane was indeed theirs. My father recalled that a search had taken place but, it was the next day before the wreck could be located. However, he could not remember on which side of the viaduct it was found.

W/Off Room told my father that the aircraft sank into the sand so fast, that divers were brought in to try and recover the pilot's body. But, it proved impossible and the aircraft became buried forcing all efforts to be abandoned after three days of continuous attempts to access the cockpit.

Account Nº 2

This account of the incident was given to me first hand by Mr Vic Shirley who was a friend of W/Off Pyka and who was in post at Walney when the crash occurred. Vic told me:

"I was a serving Corporal (Aircrew) at 10 AGS Walney when Pyka crashed and I recall the version of events that we received very well. I was present the afternoon he took off and I remember that he was in civilian clothes, just about to go on leave when he was asked to perform an air test on a Martinet which had been in for a repair. He agreed to do this and we were told that shortly after take-off and a few miles from that airfield the aircraft shed its propeller, which forced him to crash land on the sands near Ulverston.

I recall that a search was mounted but it was next day that his plane was found partly buried in soft sand but with the cockpit empty. We all believed that he had survived the crash and tried to make for the shore, only to either be drowned by the tide or sucked under the quicksand. I do recall very clearly that his body was never found".

Account Nº 3

The third and final version of the crash is concise and was given by W/Cdr Gibb to at least two sources who in turn have recounted it to me. There is no doubt that as Station Commander of RAF Cark, Jim Gibb was very "hands on" and would participate fully in all rescue operations both on site and when assistance was required further afield, so it is natural to assume that being the closest station to this crash he would automatically respond by attending with a rescue team. W/Cdr Gibbs version of the incident was as follows:

RAF Cark was notified of a crash out on the sands near the station and he took a team to search for the aircraft and pilot. Having located the wreck he made his way out to it where he found the pilot still alive but with the cockpit canopy jammed.

After struggling in vain to access the cockpit, he and his team were forced to withdraw from the scene by the rising tide. Upon returning to the site at low water the next day, the remains of the aircraft and pilot had been all but totally consumed by the soft sand. He stated that as a result of this the body of W/Off Pyka was not recovered.

**W/Off Pyka (on left)
with un-named pal
in front of Blackburn Botha
at 10 AOS Dumfries**

(courtesy of
Dumfries and Galloway
aviation museum)

Official Records (ORB's Cark Walney)

It is clear that we have conflicting versions of this tragic event and we must now look at how the incident was recorded in Walney's Operational Records book and also what details we can glean from the way it was recorded by RAF Cark.

From 10 AGS Walney we have two entries dealing with the crash, one from the station's Sick Quarters and one by the Station Commander. Walney's Sick Quarters staff operated the station ambulance and recovery/rescue team; this is their entry for the 9/11/44:

"A Martinet aircraft crashed in the estuary near Cark. The crash notification was received by flying control at 15:40 hours but the station Medical Officer was not informed by the Duty Pilot Officer until 16:21 hours. The ambulance was sent out forthwith, but the locality of the crash had been so casually defined that after several hours of fruitless search the ambulance returned. The aircraft embedded in soft mud, gradually settled down and was covered by the rising tide. It was reported some days later that Admiralty divers had been forced to suspend operations. The body of W/Off Pyka was not recovered."

From the Station Commander 10 AGS the entry for 9th November 1944 reads, "Weather – N/N Westerly wind gusty at times, visibility 20-30 miles, Fair with bright periods. Martinet HP270, the propeller and reduction gear lost in flight. Aircraft crashed in the sea just below low water mark. The pilot, W/Off PYKA was killed. Salvage operations eventually abandoned.

The Leven Estuary sands... deceptively beautiful but dangerous

Action to be taken on defective reduction gear planet wheel bearing".

The only entry we have concerning the crash from the ORB of RAF Cark is one line which reads, "10/11/44 Martinet aircraft from RAF Barrow crashed near Ulverston Viaduct, pilot killed."

To establish the actual facts surrounding this incident (as best we can), we need to examine each of the three accounts we have and set them against tidal records and ORB entries, thereby winnowing to a sufficient degree as to be sure that we are close to the truth.

Account No 1 tells us very little in any detail but does confirm the crash site as being close to Ulverston Railway viaduct. It also tells us that the wreck was not located till the following day and that divers were brought in to attempt to recover the body of W/Off Pyka but were unable to do so.

Account No 2 does give more detail with regard to the cause of the crash and tallies with official records in that the aircraft shed its propeller in flight. What cannot be correct in the way that this story found its way around 10 AGS after the event, is the idea that Pyka had escaped the crash only to drown or die in the sands. This part of the story is problematic as we know that a team of Admiralty divers toiled for at least three days before abandoning their efforts due to the wreck becoming submerged in the sand (10 AGS ORB entry). What does tally with account No 1 is the fact that C/PL Shirley remembered quite clearly that it was the day after the crash that the wreck was located.

We run into serious difficulties with account No 3 on many levels, the first being that had RAF Cark found the wreck straight away then there would have been no need for the extensive and fruitless search described in Walney's ORB. Secondly, the crash occurred late in the afternoon of a November day and by the time notification was received it would already have been growing dark. Tidal records tell us also, that high tide was at 18:41 hours on the evening of the 9th November 1944. The aircraft impacted below the low tide mark, as Walney's ORB tells us and so the tide would have been running very close to the time of the crash. It is a fact that when the ambulance team arrived in the area, having left Walney at 16:21 hours, the aircraft would probably have been completely submerged.

Low water next morning was at 01:37 hours, again during the hours of darkness and the first opportunity for a sighting of the aircraft would have been at afternoon low water which was at 13:54 hours. This confirms the suggestion that it was next day that the wreck was found, very likely as a result of an aerial search. The two questions begging answers are: If Cark's rescue team did make it to the wreck and were beaten back by the tide, why did they not inform RAF Walney's team that no further action or recovery was possible till the next day? Also, if the aircraft was upright and access to the cockpit possible, why then was extraction of the pilot not a fairly simple matter at low water the following day?

I think that the account W/Cdr Gibb gave of an attempted rescue offshore was probably not of this one and perhaps described another incident in which he was involved during his long career. We must bear in mind also, that the incident only rates a single one line entry in RAF Cark's ORB for the day and one would have expected more detail.

Conclusion and reconstruction of possible scenario

I must emphasise that the following offering is supposition only but has been constructed in the wake of discussion with several pilots, ex RAF airframe fitters and our Morecambe Bay Sand Guide, Mr Cedric Robinson.

The Miles Magister was powered by a Bristol Mercury radial engine which was encased in a substantial cowling. With the loss of the propeller of HP270, this cowling would have had a tremendous effect on the flying speed of the aircraft. Also, if further damage had occurred to the airframe due to fragmentation of the engines reduction gear casing, then the Martinet would have become very difficult to control.

W/Off Pyka is remembered as a determined and very skilled airman who would have fought his stricken aircraft to the very last and would most likely have chosen the flat sand for a belly landing, rather than water. It is possible then that he had so little control of the Martinet that no choice was available to him. With the propeller missing and with the gaping cowl to act as a water scoop, it is likely that the aircraft was thrown onto its back by the sudden deceleration. If this were indeed the case then it would explain the difficulty in reaching the pilot's body, as the operation would involve cutting through the underside of the fuselage to do so.

Miles Martinet clearly showing broad engine cowling

Almost seventy years after this tragic event we will never know the true facts for sure and all views offered by myself are purely conjecture. What we can be certain of is that both W/Off Pyka and his aircraft remain under the sands of the estuary to this day, but can we say with any certainty, where?

During the course of my investigations into the crash of the Marinet I was given a location for the crash by no less than five local people and in all five cases the general area was the same. At a place almost halfway between Cark

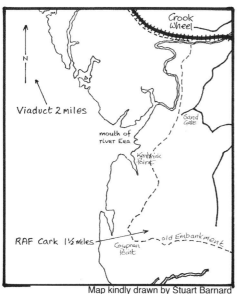

Map kindly drawn by Stuart Barnard

Airfield and the Ulverston Viaduct close to Sandgate Marsh is a point on the Ordinance Survey map marked as "Crook Wheel".

All five sources consulted agree that it is out on the sands opposite this location that the Martinet crashed. We know from official records that the aircraft went into water and I think it very likely that this water was the channel of the River Eea which runs into the sea there (see map).

The running water in this area would quite likely render the sand very unstable and would account for the rapid sinking of the aircraft over a very short period of time. In the seventy years since this incident no-one has so much as glimpsed any part of the aircraft's remains and it is likely that the wreck currently lies under a possible 1½ to 2 metres of sand, a lonely grave for a brave man a long way from his homeland.

RAF Cark was used for an emergency landing once again on the 15th November, when Halifax bomber HX292 arrived with a problem involving the aircraft's starboard outer engine. Repairs were carried out by a servicing party and the Halifax left for its home base some forty-eight hours later. For a while discussion had been taking place with regard to the relocation of 650 Squadron and the departure of the Royal Artilleries Anti-Aircraft batteries. Official confirmation was received and the Martinets and Hurricanes of 650 Squadron began to leave for their new base at RAF Bodorgan, Anglesey on the 18th of the month. As the Royal Artillery slowly left I am told that the slumbering pilots on stand down from night flying duties did not mourn their passing!

Instrument section staff 1944

December came and went with no mishap and Christmas was celebrated in the usual manner. However, with the new year came a new role for RAF Cark and one that they would fill before January 1945 was through. On the 2nd January, several miles up the west coast at RAF Millom, all flying abruptly ceased following a notice from Training Command that the station's services were no longer required. In post at Millom were the station's officially recognised and highly efficient Mountain Rescue unit, who were now in need of a base close to the Lakeland fells. As Millom was placed under Care and Maintenance and only a skeleton staff left to care for the site, all mountain rescue personnel and equipment were transferred to RAF Cark. The base officially assumed main mountain rescue responsibilities for the area, on the 11th of the month. One of the RAF's most experienced mountain rescue staff was Flt/Lt John (Doc) Lloyd; an officer who had gained much experience whilst working with the well-established team at RAF Llandwrog on Anglesey, before being transferred to RAF Millom. Flt/Lt Lloyd was also posted in as Medical Officer in overall charge of the Cark team and had barely had time to settle in when his party were called to attend their first crash on the 17th January and only six days into their new posting.

November 1944 one of No9 light artillery unit's 40mm Bofors guns awaits transfer from RAF Cark

One of 650 squadron's Defiants had remained on station up to this point due to what I believe were mechanical problems seen here in November 1944. It was flown out to a maintenance unit as the squadron left and subsequently struck off charge

Nº 46 Course

Back L to R – F/Lt Kelly, Sgts Niedzwiecki, Drzewicki, Drzewicki, W/O Janik, Sgt Hewitt, F/Sgt Higgs, Sgt Mitchell, F/Sgts Abbott, Gater
Middle L to R – Sgts Murdoch, Bonsey, Adams, Bosley, Browne F/Sgt Kerney, F/O McWatt, F/Os Hill, Mack
Front L to R – F/Lt Parks, F/Os Wheatly, Wright P/Os Goode, Legg, F/Os Barker, Harries, Walby, Byford, Dobson

Nº 47 Course

Back L to R – Sgt Browning, Barr, Hutton, Lawrenson, Hall, Luff, F/Sgts Mutters, Wynd, Evans, Sgt Harrison
Middle L to R – F/Os Wilson, Sutherland, Sgts Brown, Banbury, F/Os Clements, Ullyett, F/Lt Allan, Sgt Cockham, F/O Straight, Sgt McGregor, F/Os Noble, Jones
Front L to R – Sgts Milligan, Atwill, F/Sgts Darling, Robinson, F/Os Dean, Wolfe Ryan, Barcroft, Jeffery-Cridge, Sgt Kemp

Nº 48 Course

Back L to R – F/Sgt WcEvoy, Sgts Siddall, Barber, Turnbull, F/Sgt Foot, Sgts Meadows, Dewhurst, Andrews, F/Sgt Jameson, P/O Knapp, F/Sgt Guy, F/O Keen, Sgt Hickson
Middle L to R – F/Sgt Jones, Sgts Lloyd-Jones, *unknown, unknown, unknown*, F/Sgt Frost, Sgts Henderson, Harvey, F/Sgts Milne, Fry, *unknown*
Front L to R – Sgts Stonelake, Llewellyn, W/O Vasey, F/O Kay, F/Lt Foster-Packer, P/O Belt, F/Lt Mc Leod, F/Os Miners, Sharp, Russell, Sgt Percy-Smith

Nº 49 Course

Back L to R – Sgts Hyett, Smith RE Henderson, Kozadiewicz, Coleman, Cousins, CambelL F/Sgt Dewar, Sgts Chilcot, Burrow
Middle L to R – P/O Hinsworth, F/O Franczak, Sgts Smith T Revell Beller, Caldwell, Collins, Box, F/Sgt Reid, Sgts Berriman, Carr
Front L to R – P/Os Alderton, Digby-Seymour, Streatfield, F/O Venn, F/Lt Lowe, F/O Baxter, F/Os Marsh, Johnston, Carr, P/O Williams, F/O Dickson

Nº 50 Course

Back L to R – F/Sgt Evans, F/O Crook, Sgt Lewis, F/Sgt Douglas, F/O Stacey, F/Sgts Rimmer, Seymour, Sgt Taylor, F/Os Wray, Looker, Oldcorn
Middle L to R – F/Sgts Scott, Rock, Sgt Smetham, F/Sgt Hammond, Sgt Davey, F/Sgt Gillatt, Sgt Fox, F/Sgts Thomas, Nicol, Ferguson, F/O Purvis
Front L to R – Sgts Ding, Ford, Hall, Murton, W/O Hall, P/O Legg, F/Lt Henkel, Sgt Baxter, F/O Barrett, Mayor

Nº 51 Course

Back L to R – W/O Barnett, F/Sgt Grafton, Sgts Fullick, Winser, Blackadder, Herbert, F/Os Carroll PA Carroll LC Haworth, Broom
Middle L to R – F/O Woodburn, Sgts Pulling, Smithers, Barrass, F/Sgt Meikle, Sgts Wilson, Smith, F/Os Watt Howard
Front L to R – F/Os Yeoman, Hurwitz, Poynter, Pearce, Law, W/O Renshaw, F/Os Holmes, Richardson, Binns, Williams

At around 14:00 hours that day, word arrived at Cark that a Grumman Avenger torpedo bomber on exercise from RNAS Inskip had crashed above Wastwater and the team set out to search for the crash site. After an all-night search the wreck was located high up on the Wastwater screes; all three crewmen were dead and the aircraft totally destroyed.

Whilst this tragedy was unfolding, back at Cark, Staff Pilot course No 49 had been completed. As the course members awaited their respective postings, course No 53 arrived to begin training, though not in the best of weather conditions as the station's ORB records very low temperatures and several inches of snow. In spite of this, the airfield was kept operational with only one

Grumman Avenger 1:72 scale model

accident; Anson LT237 overshot on landing and lost both undercarriage units, happily there were no casualties.

The cold spell continued with a further six inches of snow on the 29th, but

Flare pistol from Wasdale Avenger found on screes by the late Mr M.Dixon whilst walking there a few weeks after the crash

again the airfield was kept operational until the next day when much of the snowfall began to thaw due to a rise in temperature, accompanied by rain and drizzle. January ended with the completion of No 50 Staff Pilots course on the 30th and the arrival of No 54 course intake on the 31st ; flying continued in spite of the difficult weather conditions.

Nº 52 Course
Back L to R – Beckett, Burakouski, Maismer, Beiley, Johnstone, Tiplady, Kendrick, Lytile, Szvmanski, Glandfield, Jackson
Middle L to R – Stark, Frid, Bass, Carpenter, Moriarty, Clifford, Couch, Eke, Stephenson, Young, Leech, Ford
Front L to R – Hunt, Levette, F/L Frame, F/O Cameron, F/O Parkinson (staff), F/L McGruddon, F/O Carder, P/O Wilkinson, Parry, Dixer

Nº 53 Course
Back L to R
F/S Noon, F/S Costella, S Bremer, F/S McBride, F/S Duffy, P/O Jackson Moore, F/O Fennell, F/O Harper, F/S Jupp, F/O Jennison, F/O Jones
Middle L to R
F/O Cosack, F/S Kessell, F/S Ward, F/O Chillman, F/S Paul, F/S Cooper, F/O Davidson, F/S Exelby, F/S Young, F/S Walker, F/S Ewth
Front L to R – F/O Brett, S.Holloway, F/S Hardy, F/L Atkins, P/O Cost, F/L Lewis, F/O Atkinson, F/S Gray, F/S Killen, S.Donnelly

Nº 54 Course

Back L to R – F/O Gill, F/S Holmes, S.Harris, F/O Oldacre, S.Turpin, S.Worgan, Leavey, F/S Southgate, F/S Holly, F/S Lynar

Middle L to R – F/S Seaton, STeague, F/O Ireland, F/O Payne, W/O Castles, SHaynes, F/S Walker, F/S Teagueew, F/S Dobson, F/S Lalor, F/O McLaren

Front L to R – F/S Parsons, F/O Ruffle, F/O Sharpe, S.Russill, F/S Mearill, P/O Thompson, F/S Stoddart, F/O Hitzke, F/O Carrick, F/S Corloran

Nº 55 Course

Back L to R – F/S Smith, F/S Wright, F/S Tayler, Sgts Webb, Chelin, Parkinson, Eagle, Cooper, F/S Keetuey, F/S Greenham, Sgt Archer

Middle L to R – F/S Spires, Sgts Mc Pherson, White, Wood, Re-veet, F/O Dawson, F/O Smellie, P/O Hubbard, F/O Biggs, F/O Shapman, Sgt Evans, F/S McLaughlin

Front L to R – F/S Ward, F/S Thorne, F/S Carter, F/L Haines, Sgt Lee, F/O Dodgson, F/S Geeson, F/S Price, F/S Armstrong

On the 7th February Cark received a visit from SGT Hans Pick who was to spend nine days at the unit giving further instruction to their mountain rescue team. SGT Pick was a refugee from his native Austria and had served in the Alpine Division of the Austrian Army. He was an accomplished climber and author of climbing guide books prior to hostilities and his departure from his homeland. Now he was in the British Army, seconded to the RAF as a mountain rescue instructor. His task was to tour the growing number of teams and develop their mountaineering skills as required.

Three days after his arrival he was to accompany the Cark team who were called to attend the crash site of Mosquito HK141 on the slopes above Red Tarn on Hellvellyn. The aircraft had been on exercise from No 51 OTU Cranfield and both crewmen were found to have been killed upon impact, in what was a head on collision with the fellside.

DH Mosquito

Red Tarn is one of the deepest mountain tarns in the Lakeland fells and it is said that the two Merlin engines from the Mosquito, along with more heavy wreckage, was pushed out onto the surface of the tarn which was frozen at the time of the crash. With a thaw, the said items would sink into its icy depths and save much work for the MU tasked with cleaning the site. It is entirely possible that this was indeed the case. Further credence is given to this version of events by the fact that recreational divers, who have ventured some way below the surface of this very deep and cold little body of water, have recovered various metal airframe components.

Only three days after the Helvellyn crash the team were called out once again, this time across the border into Yorkshire where a Mustang fighter aircraft had crashed. The scene of the accident was at High Bentham and once again the team were confronted with a fatality. The Mustang was outbound on a training exercise from No 61 OTU Rodnal, Salop. Its Polish pilot had been killed instantly from multiple injuries, leaving the team once again with the grisly task of recovering the body of the airman and arranging transport for him back to his parent unit.

Such was the task for many of the occasions upon which the team was called out. So, it must have been with some relief that when called upon once more on 15th February to attend a crash on the outskirts of Cark, they found an uninjured crew standing with their stricken aircraft.

Following complete loss of power and unable to reach RAF Cark's runways for an emergency landing, Anson MG963 flying from RAF Wigtown crash landed in the fields by Wraysholme Railway crossing. It came to rest leaving all four crew members shaken but safe. A short sprint for the team and a happy outcome!

We can be sure that by this time captured Italian prisoners were working at RAF Cark carrying out manual work etc, because on the 21st February the station received a visit from Lt/Col F.R. Palengat. He was there in his capacity as War Office Inspector of Prisoners of War and left satisfied with the overall attitude of and work conditions for, Cark's Italian "co-operators".

The weather for February is logged in the airfield's records as, "Very poor with much ground mist and at times dense fog". Also mentioned are three days of extreme gale force winds, which when combined with restricted visibility throughout the month, was to cut down flying hours to the extent that they go unrecorded.

On the 6th March 1945 No 52 Staff Pilots course was completed with an output of three Officers and twenty-seven Non Commissioned Officers. The very next day the intake of course No 56 comprised of twelve Officers and 18 NCOs. This demonstrates quite clearly that even at this late stage of the war, training continued at the same pace.

On the 17th of the month at 22:35 hours, Halifax bomber LW575 made an emergency landing at Cark, having sustained serious damage by enemy machine gun fire during an operational flight. One crew member had been injured during the attack and he was taken by ambulance to Conishead Priory Hospital, Ulverston. Repairs to the aircraft were deemed to be beyond unit resources and were carried out by No 75 MU. The aircraft was returned to its parent unit of RAF Dishforth some days later.

On the 20th March No 53 course was completed and the very next day No 57 course commenced training in excellent weather. The station ORB stating at the month's end, "Four outstanding weeks of flying weather with much higher than normal temperatures for the time of year".

As April began and training continued, there was much speculation throughout the country as to when the war in Europe would be brought to an end. With the allies moving ever closer to the German capital and victory in sight, it must surely have been felt that news would be heard within weeks, if not days. It was to be on the 30th April during the final apocalyptic battle for Berlin that Hitler's death was announced. Having appointed Admiral

Karl Doenitz his successor, Hitler committed suicide in his bunker leaving Doenitz and the defeated German people to their fate.

On the 7th May 1945 in Reims, France, an act of military surrender was signed by Admiral Doenitz and ratified on the 8th May 1945 in Berlin. Across Britain and beyond, V.E. day celebrations began. However, the war in the Far East was far from over and there was no clear indication as to how much longer the dogged Japanese would continue to endure all the gathered military might now being thrown against them.

On the 30th May No 58 Staff Pilot course was completed and its Officers and NCOs sent on leave to return for further instruction and postings to their new units. Weather was recorded as mixed during the month but conducive to flying training, with several clear days and light winds.

With outright victory now a clear possibility for the allies in the near future, the Government's thoughts were turning to settlement and employment plans for the huge amount of military personnel who would be released from service at the close of hostilities. On the 4th June a speaker from the Ministry of Labour visited Cark and delivered a series of lectures on these matters. They were well received and must have been thought provoking for many as they contemplated an abrupt return to civilian life in the not too distant future.

RAF Cark's gymnasium set for celebration!

The use of dogs in rescue situations is taken for granted these days, but they had never been experimented with by the RAF Mountain Rescue teams, until trials were carried out by Cark on the 28th June 1945. At 08:00 hours that day, Grp/Cpt Gregor FTC, Sq/Ldr McDowell, F/Lt Gill, F/Lt Baird, F/Lt McDonnel, Col Baldwin, Lt/Col Dave and W/Off Hans Pick arrived to carry out a series of exercises using trained dogs to assess their suitability in this capacity. The team were delighted with the results and the role of the search dog was cemented into RAF Mountain Rescue from that time to the present day.

At 10:55 hours on the 30th June the station's rescue team were called out once again when word arrived that a horrific crash had occurred at Crosthwaite in Westmorland. An aircraft was seen circling the village with

Crosthwaite vicarage (present day)

smoke trailing behind it and with its engine misfiring very badly at around 10:30 hours that morning. Unable to maintain altitude or find an area to land, the aircraft struck trees behind the village vicarage before hitting the vicarage roof losing a portion of its port wing. The wrecked aircraft then crashed into the adjacent road and burst into flames.

Upon hearing the crash and the sound of exploding munitions, the landlord of the village public house ran to the scene and was able to remove the pilot from the burning wreck. This was to no avail however as the pilot, 2nd L/T E.W. Kortendick had been killed on impact. The aircraft was a Mustang on exercise from U.S. Army Air Station Honington when it developed engine problems. The incident must have been a traumatic and upsetting one for the small community of Crossthwaite.

July saw the final two courses pass out of Cark, Staff Pilot Course No 60 on 15th of the month and an all French Course (no number allocated) on the 21st. As the month came and went, an event was about to take place which would not only end WWII, but one which would change the world forever.

On the 6th August 1945, from the Battle Cruiser U.S.S. Augusta in the Mid Atlantic, American President Harry S. Truman announced to the world that a B29 Superfortress had dropped an atomic bomb on the Japanese city of Hiroshima, bringing about its total destruction. The bomb represented a destructive capability some two thousand times in excess of any weapon used up to that point in the conflict and the world looked on in awe.

At controls of Anson
RAF Cark

F/S Dobson with 2 pals RAF

Len with Anson
RAF Jurby

RAF Cark

1944 a young flight sergeant named Len Dobson attended Course No 54 at RAF Cark. He left us with a glimpse into his time training and his subsequent posting to 5AOS Jurby IOM

Air-to-air over Isle of M

Three days later and with no clear indication that Japan was about to surrender immediately, the Americans unleashed the same devastation on the town of Nagasaki, once again bringing about its total destruction. The inevitable happened officially on the 15th August 1945, when it was announced that Japan had finally surrendered, the war was at last over.

As I sit at my desk and pen this in April 2012 and with the world seeking a lasting peace from all the smaller, but equally destructive wars which currently rage around our world, the words of Winston Churchill, spoken in the wake of Hiroshima and Nagasaki come to mind. He said "We must indeed pray that these awful agencies will be made to conduce peace among the nations and that instead of wreaking havoc upon the entire globe they become a perennial fountain of world prosperity".

A noble sentiment and a sincere hope on behalf of Winston Churchill I am sure and it is a fact that the existence of nuclear weapons has prevented a global conflict up until the present day. There is a less than subtle irony, is there not however, in using the annihilation of mankind and the threat of destruction of almost every living thing on earth as a vehicle to ensure peace?

And so Cark's gymnasium was once again the scene of celebration. Then with V J Day come and gone, the station began to slow down and settle in to the new peace. As August progressed several of Cark's now surplus aircraft began to leave for pastures new, along with a good number of personnel; the station's life was drawing to a close.

W/Cdr Gibb with officers and flying staff - 1944
(The station flagpole can be seen to this present day though now recumbent!)

Nº 56 Course
Back L to R – Sgts Rauw, Anczutin, Finch, Ellis, Shill, F/S Cawston, Sgts McMaster, Hynds, F/S Spencer
Middle L to R – P/O Simpson, Sgts Maybee, McPhee, F/S Wallace, Sgts Jeffrey, Brooks, W/O Ross, Sgts Bradbury, Mann, F/O Spencer
Front L to R – F/Os Baker, Friggens, Keasbeck, Kula, Baxter, P/O Mastin, F/Os Bokowiak, Ruddle, Venthara, Lauder

Nº 57 Course
Back L to R – F/S Jones, F/S Kemp, F/S Markie, F/S Dick, W/O Williams, F/S Bright, Sgt Cook
Middle L to R – F/S Austin, F/S Harwood, F/S Holland, F/S Phelps, F/S Irving, F/S Killick, F/S Horsey, F/S Fry
Front L to R – F/S Williams, F/S Cotton, F/O Clutton, F/O Linnegar, F/O Cust, F/O Shellard, P/O Storey, P/O Smith, W/O Dyball

Nº 58 Course

Back L to R – Hardy, Stell, Wade, Duncan, Bowland, Drew, Goff, Rounthwaite, Brozek, Jankowski
Middle L to R – Taylor, Munro, King, Smith, Mitchell, Kiff, Anderson, Habbick, Gore, Romanes, Wastell
Front L to R – Wyver, Clark, Brunton, Hood, Wilson, Lisney, Snowden, Bold, Carpanini, Morek

Nº 59 Course

Back L to R – F/S Catterill, F/S McSorland, Sgt Hall, Sgt Kirkwood, Sgt Tait, F/S Jackson, Sgt Leighton, F/S Clarke, Sgt Pickup, Sgt Rogers
Middle L to R – F/O Inch, Sgt Long, F/O Jones, P/O Tucker, F/O Heptonstall, F/O Smith, F/O Terrell, Sgt Box, F/S Clifford, Sgt Marsden
Front L to R – P/O Roberts, P/O Ralph, F/O Emmett, F/O Lisney, P/O Whiteoak, F/O Robbie, F/O McGregor, F/O Spofforth, F/O Cockerill

Nº 60 Course - May 1945
Back L to R – Sgt Mason Sgt Bryce, F/S Bullen, Sgt Butterworth, Sgt Dugdale,Sgt Hemsley, Sgt Anderson, Sgt Tucker, F/S Townsend, Sgt Jeffery
Middle L to R – Sgt Lacey, F/O Amey, P/O Smith, P/O Jackson, P/O King, F/O Wise, F/O Mitchell, Sgt Banks, Sgt Tector, P/O Pratchett, Sgt Lee
Front L to R – F/O Hyde, F/O Millar, F/Lt Jones, F/O Cust, F/O Bartup, F/O Munro, F/O Paxton, W/O Hardwick

French Course - July 1945
Back L to R – ASPt Cahouet, S/Lt Contri, Lt Ayme, F/O Dean, Capt Jorgensen Lt Cognet, S/Lt Gavignet
Front L to R – Sgts Deleon Chaffenet, Letroublon, Lhenry, Tiphine, Aperce, Derenne

RAF Cark was not about to slip away quietly however and on the 15ᵗʰ September the station held on "RAF at home day". This was in effect a celebratory air show and was well attended by nearly three thousand people from the surrounding counties. The unit's diary tells us that the aircraft displayed were: Harvard, Mosquito, Oxford, Tempest, Spitfire, Wellington, Anson, Halifax and Lancaster. £20 was raised for the RAF Benevolent Fund. The rest of September's station diary entries concern weather conditions and visits by various officers and agencies concerning personnel postings, resettlement and eventual closure of the unit.

This trend continues through October and November into December until the 15ᵗʰ of that month when the unit was called to attend and leave a guard on a crashed aircraft which had come to grief on Whernside in Yorkshire (close to Ribblehead Railway Station). The aircraft in question was Barracuda DR306 of RNAS Rattray and its pilot P/O JR Crevier escaped with minor injuries.

In terms of details and information over the last two weeks of December, the station's Operational Records Book is virtually barren and concludes on the 31ˢᵗ December 1945 with this one line entry, "No 1 SPTU disbanded, station placed under Care and Maintenance".

Cark airfield has seen usage of various types between its closure and the present day: go-kart race track, pasture, motorcycle race track, to name but a few. Latterly it's the home of a parachute school and plays host to the annual 'Flookburgh Steam Gathering', Cark airfield didn't die it just took a nap!

Front-centre, W/Off Gibb with 17 members of original Cark staff from 1942 posed in front of station commander's Magister at close of station (1945)

RAF Cark – Part 2
Accounts of some who served at RAF Cark

Having concluded a précis of the history of RAF Cark in so much as it was officially recorded it is time now to move on finally to the personal accounts,

anecdotes and recollections contributed by those who served there during the station's wartime life. Three of these accounts are best described as semi-autobiographical in content. They provide comprehensive details of life both on and off the unit and the duties carried out by its personnel. When I first began my research I was curious about the background of the overseas trainees who arrived at RAF Cark, RAF Millom and units like it. What drove these men and women who came across the globe to take up the fight against the axis powers? What sort of characters were they? And what course did their lives take on return to their home countries?

Authors Disclaimer The opinions expressed in the following accounts are those of the contributors and do not necessarily represent those of the author.

Mr I. Bain – Cark 1943

My log-book tells me that I was stationed at the Staff Pilot Training Unit, Cark, from November 16th to December 30th, 1943. It was not a happy posting. Having signed up to go anywhere and do anything for King and Country, I – along with virtually all the aircrew in the Course – was bitterly disappointed (and more than a little embarrassed) by being relegated to the flying of trainee navigators around the Irish Sea in effing Ansons.

I am sure that the Lake District lives up to its reputation as one of the premier beauty spots of Britain in summer, in winter, even the few Canadians on the Course who were accustomed to very-much-below-zero winter weather 'back home' found the Cark winter to be miserably damp and bone-chillingly cold. The Nissen huts we used as living-quarters were 'heated' by a tiny stove in the middle of the room in which we burned any unattached wooden objects and a few pieces of coal from the normally well- guarded pile. As I recall, we often slept fully clothed – and in flying suits – and more often than not, we had only cold water for our ablutions.

I will enclose copies of pages from my log-book to indicate the kind of flying exercises we were engaged in. Unfortunately, I cannot recall what the various references mean in ordinary English but you may be able to find a local interpreter! One entry suggests that I landed from about 20 feet – described as being "rough". That would have been an understatement if true but I do remember one occasion – at night – when I misjudged my height and thought that I would be wearing the undercarriage around my neck when we stopped bouncing.

As frightening as that heavy landing was for me and those flying with me, it was not as serious a risk as the night when I was what seemed like inches from a collision with another aircraft. The practice was for aircraft to take off on a pre-determined schedule, climb to a designated height and then fly over the airfield setting the designated course. It was not anticipated that delays would lead to two aircraft planning to set course over the airfield at the same time!

On this occasion, as I was getting ready to set course on our trip, I noticed the lights of another aircraft off to my port side. It can be difficult at night to positively determine just where the other aircraft is and what the pilot intends doing. Within seconds, it became apparent that the other aircraft was drifting in my direction and at approximately the same altitude. As I pointed the nose of my aircraft sharply down, the other pilot pulled his up and I braced for the sound and feel of metal on metal as we passed. When we assembled in the briefing–room after the flight, a pilot – obviously the other pilot – stood up and in shockingly obscene terms described what had happened and challenged the offending pilot to identify himself. Fat chance!

On happier note – local families in the area were very generous with their hospitality and I remember one pleasant occasion when several of the men on my course were invited to an evening with a local pub owner and his family in their living quarters above the pub. Their daughter had invited several other local girls and with food, beverage and music it was really as close to a family occasion as the airmen – especially the Colonials – would enjoy during their stay in Britain.

Ian Bain

(2012)

Log page courtesy of Mr I.Bain from his time at RAF Cark

YEAR 1943		AIRCRAFT		PILOT, OR 1ST PILOT	2ND PILOT, PUPIL OR PASSENGER	DUTY (INCLUDING RESULTS AND REMARKS
MONTH	DATE	Type	No.			
—	—	—	—	—	—	—
						TOTALS BROUGHT FORWA
DEC	11	ANSON	EG637	P/o SMITH	SGT. BURTON SELF	X-COUNTRY (PILOT) NIGHT
"	11	ANSON	EG637	P/o SMITH	SGT. BURTON SELF	X-COUNTRY (NAVIGATOR)
"	13	ANSON	MG227	SGT MUDDELL	SGT. CASTLE SELF	Q.G.H.
"	13	ANSON	MG227	SGT MUDDELL	SGT. CASTLE SELF	PASSENGER (Q.G.H.)
"	17	ANSON	MG227	SELF	SGT. BIFFEN	X-COUNTRY (PILOT) NIGHT
"	19	ANSON	MG227	SGT HAYES	SELF	X-COUNTRY (NAVIGATOR)
"	20	ANSON	MG234	SELF	SGT BLAIR W/OP SGT BIFFEN	X-COUNTRY (PILOT)
"	22	ANSON	LT189	F/o CLARKSON	SGT HAYES SELF	X-COUNTRY (NAV.) NIGHT
"	22	ANSON	LT427	F/o BARLOW	F/S BENNETT F/S BALL SGT. BLAIR	X-COUNTRY (PILOT)
"	23	ANSON	LT427	F/o ROUSE	F/S BENNETT SELF	X-COUNTRY (NAV). NIGHT
"	23	ANSON	LT427	F/o ROUSE	F/S BENNETT SELF	X-COUNTRY (PILOT) NIGHT
"	27	ANSON	EG700	F/o ROUSE	F/S TRENDALL SELF	X-COUNTRY (NAV.)

Rob Clarkson F/o
OC FLIGHT

C.C. Price I/C
CFI. S.P.T.U

SUMMARY FOR S.P.T.U. COURSE   1. ANSO

UNIT: S.P.T.U

DATE: DEC. 29, 1943

SIGNATURE *W.J.Bain* SGT

GRAND TOTAL [Cols. (1) to (10)]

368 Hrs. 00 Mins.

TOTALS CARRIED FORW

SINGLE-ENGINE AIRCRAFT				MULTI-ENGINE AIRCRAFT						PASS-ENGER	INSTR/CLOUD FLYING [Incl. in cols. (1) to (10)]		LINK TRAINER
DAY		NIGHT		DAY			NIGHT						
DUAL	PILOT	DUAL	PILOT	DUAL	1ST PILOT	2ND PILOT	DUAL	1ST PILOT	2ND PILOT		DUAL	PILOT	
(1)	(2)	(3)	(4)	(5)	(6)	(7)	(8)	(9)	(10)	(11)	(12)	(13)	(14)
8·30	30·00	04:00		133:15	99:00		23·20	23:55		51·40	55·15		37·00

(*11212, Wt. 40572—2665 20,000 1/43 T.S. **700**
(*12278—11212) Wt. 15036—517 50M 6/43 T.S. **700** — No 26 COURSE — FORM 414 (A)

SUMMARY of FLYING and ASSESSMENTS FOR ~~YEAR COMMENCING~~ 1st *19x3

[* For Officer, insert "JUNE" ; For Airman Pilot, insert "AUGUST."]

	S.E. AIRCRAFT		M.E. AIRCRAFT		TOTAL for year	GRAND TOTAL All Service Flying
	Day	Night	Day	Night		
DUAL	—	—	6.00	2.30	8.30	
PILOT	—	—	15.05	12.00	27.05	
~~PASSENGER~~ NAVIGATOR	—				21.55.	

ASSESSMENT of ABILITY

(To be assessed as :—Exceptional, Above the Average, Average)

(i) AS A STAFF † PILOT... Average

(ii) AS ~~PILOT-NAVIGATOR~~/NAVIGATOR... Average

(iii) IN BOMBING...

(iv) IN AIR GUNNERY...

(v) IN S.B.A...

Insert :—"F.", "L.B.", "G.R.", "F.B.", "Instructor", etc.

ANY POINTS IN FLYING OR AIRMANSHIP WHICH SHOULD BE WATCHED

— Nil —

Date 29/12/43   Signature P.C.Price S/LDR
for Officer Commanding... S.A.T.U. CARK.

CERTIFIED THAT I HAVE BEEN INSTRUCTED IN ANSON DINGHY DRILL AND HAVE COMPLETED 2 Q.G.H. EXERCISES.

W.J.Bain Sgt.

| 13·30 | 30:00 | 04:00 | | 133:15 | 106:00 | | 23:20 | 32:55 | | 66:50 | 55:15 | | |
| (1) | (2) | (3) | (4) | (5) | (6) | (7) | (8) | (9) | (10) | (11) | (12) | (13) | (14) |

Mr Ross Blanchard — 1944 – 1945

I have a very strong belief that I was a gleam in my mother and fathers eyes about Christmas 1922 or New Year 1923, for I arrived on the scene about 17:30 hrs Western Standard time on the 28th September 1923 at Hay Street, West Perth, Western Australia. I have absolutely no recollections of this very important occasion!! My mother used to tell me, some years later, that she had to be very careful to keep our front gate shut; otherwise I would get out and run like crazy down Hay Street with her in hot pursuit! I have only two memories of this period, and both of these were on board the steamship which took us to live in Wellington New Zealand in early 1927.

A young Ross 'pilots' his first craft

The first of these recollections was of me being a bit cheeky to one of the crew, and as a gesture to get me back in order he grabbed me by the ankles and held me over the side of the ship. I was very excited at the sight of the white waves whistling past below, with absolutely no fear, but a little bit sad as my halfpenny personal fortune slipped out of my pocket and disappeared forever in the ocean depths. My second memory is of my sister Margaret and her girlfriend enticing me into a game of chasing. I had almost caught the pair of them when one of them slammed the cabin door shut, and sadly for me, one of my fingers got trapped in it. It hurt like hell, but it was one of my very first lessons about pursuing members of the opposite sex!!

I believe we arrived in New Zealand early in 1927, and stayed at the Oriental Hotel on the South side of Wellington harbour. My father had been appointed as the minister of Saint John's Presbyterian Church, where he stayed until late August 1939. Soon after our arrival my mother took us on holiday to one of the Eastern harbour beaches, and it was there, following a horrible experience that my fear of dogs began, and it took me a long time to overcome it!

About this time, work on the building of the new Presbyterian Church was well under way, and on my first visit I was amazed that there was no visible connection between the ground floor and the upstairs. This was very easily explained to me by my father (stairs come later!) My schooling started at

Primary School, I think in 1928, with a fairly long walk each way, doing my best to avoid being bitten by dogs!! I remember very vividly two experiences whilst at this school of learning, the first being watching the senior boys climbing a wall at the back of the school building, the wall going from ground level up to a great height, then back to ground level. This wall was about a foot wide and backed by a corrugated iron fence, and the senior boys made it look very easy, so I figured it they can do it, so can I! Well, I got to the top OK, but then I just froze with not a clue what to do next. My situation created a great deal of interest amongst the other kids and one female teacher. I finished up jumping off and instead of landing on my toes, it was the flat of my feet that took the blow and it hurt! Apparently I went white in the face, and the teacher asked me if I was alright. Being a very independent character I said yes, and walked away as best I could. It took many years to find out that this prang had caused a curvature of my spine which has remained with me all my days, through fortunately, three or four treatments a year by a chiropractor of excellent quality keeps me in reasonable shape. I have examined that wall in recent years and came to the conclusion that I must have been round the bend to jump off it, there's no way I would have done it again!

The second incident – concerned a girl student who was screaming her head off at me for walking in an out of bounds area. Now, because she was so insistent and so loud I got pretty rattled, and looking around I saw an old horseshoe lying not far away from me which I thought would be a great thing to scare her off and make her shut up. I picked it up and threw it at her with the intention of giving her the fright of her life. Unfortunately my aim was first class with a bull's-eye score followed by immediate silence. I was horrified and not knowing what to do left the scene as quickly as possible. I was  summoned by the head mistress later that day and given a letter to take to my parents when I got home. Being an idiot, I shoved the letter into a post box on my way home with no clear strategy in mind at all. I was lucky I never heard another thing about it!

In 1930 I became a student at Scots College situated in a southern suburb of Wellington. I was never happy at this school and though I won most of my weight for age bouts in the boxing ring I seemed to be number one target for the oafish bullies the school was riddled with. My best mate at this time was Barney Hope Gibbons, whose dad was a very wealthy Ford Motor car dealer, we had many adventures. In 1936 my 13th birthday present was a B.S.A. Bicycle, very heavy, no gears and no handbrakes, but I thought it was marvellous and used it to cycle the five miles to school every day irrespective of the weather. By 1939 I was a member of the third fifteen rugby football team and we set a record by winning all our games that season! I was also to receive my one and only trophy from the school that same year when I won the intermediate boxing championship. I started my second term holiday in August and spent it skiing at Tongarino National Park and having a great time. I then travelled solo to Auckland by train and stayed with some family friends before sailing to Sydney Australia and my home country. The trip was made under blackout conditions and this was to be my first taste of the nasty forthcoming wartime restrictions. My stay in Sydney was spent with my Uncle Louis who was also a Presbyterian Minister and it was a marvellous family reunion.

I returned to restart my education at Scotch College, Torrens Park in October arriving for my first day by train with many other 'new starters'. Very soon after my arrival of my new school I was cornered by a group of lads in the quadrangle and subjected to some tough questioning. With each question the group got closer and closer making it clear that they were 'checking me out'. Before I was the subject of any physical contest I very quietly mentioned that I had just won the intermediate boxing championship at my last school. The effect was immediate with several backwards steps all round, and facial expressions which said, 'we think we'd better show this bloke a bit of respect'. From that moment on I never experienced any problems at all at this college. 1939 finished with a holiday at Encounter Bay, about 60 miles south of Adelaide, with my mother and my younger sister Lesley. We enjoyed lots of walking and surfing at a fairly isolated beach which has since been put under warning, having claimed many lives over the years due to the sometimes dangerous conditions.

1940 – 1942 I truly enjoyed my 2 years and three months at Scotch College largely because of the sporting opportunities which were, Australian Rules football, swimming, athletics, cross country running, boxing and gymnastics. I ended my time at the College with quite a few records and trophies. The first was for breaking the mile run record time which had stood for 20 years! I also narrowly missed breaking the schools 880 yard record when I ran in just under a 1/5th of a second short of the schools previous best. I left the College in 1941 but I have a vivid memory whilst there, of a speech given to all the boys by our Headmaster on the day that the French capitulated. His name was Mr Norman Gratton and he told us that in spite of these events, "I do not know how or when, but I am convinced that the British will win this war"! This set me thinking straight away for being only a couple of months away from my seventeenth birthday it was quite obvious that I would be involved one way or another.

Now, having been in the army cadet corps at both schools I had no desire to continue in that service. The thought of being at sea for up to nine months at a stretch without any female company was just not on! This left the air force, and if I was going to volunteer then it would be for aircrew training with the R.A.A.F. I spoke to my parents about the matter and they agreed to give their written consent when I had finished my year at college. You can imagine my excitement when I finally got that "piece of paper"! and with my parents blessings in my pocket I cycled out of our front gate on my way to "join up"! As I did so a man walked past and yelled in a very loud voice"the Japs have bombed Pearl Harbour". I gave him a wave to acknowledge his message, wondering where on earth Pearl Harbour was, and came to the conclusion that with a name like that it must be American and possibly in the Aleutian Islands. Correct on number one but wrong on number two! I arrived at the R.A.A.F. recruiting office on North Terrace, Adelaide and made an apology that I could not be available for the next two weeks as my parents were insisting that I finish my schooling. He gave quite a chuckle, put one arm round my shoulder and said "don't worry son, we're inundated with applicants, you won't be called up for at least six or seven months", and he was right, the date was the 18th July 1942. And so I had to wait my turn!

I made a couple of good mates around this time, one of whom was Paul Kennett, we used to cycle to school together all the time smoking furiously! Paul and I loved Jazz music and I remember after the final curtain at a concert we attended, leaping onto the stage with Paul and the pair of us jitterbugging madly to two 78 records, Sweet You Just You' by Joe Daniells and his hot shots in Drumnastics, and 'Dusk in Upper Sandusky' by the Ray McKinley Orchestra. I was hooked!! In fact I was so hooked I went on to take drumming lessons from the late Mr Dick Smith who was the timpanist with the Adelaide Symphony Orchestra. I needed some work as I waited for my call up to come and so I took employment with Woodroofes, the soft drink makers and managed to stick it for a month! Next I got a job as a driver with Yellow Cabs, this lasted three months and I learnt more about the human race in this time than I had in all of my previous years, it was a magnificent occupation but I had a bit of stoush with one of the administrators and left. My final short stint of civilian employment was as a mechanic with Silver Taxis, and that too was educational! During this time I was called up for a medical test to go into the army. This was the compulsory service and was known to us all as the "chocolate soldiers" and was not optional! Anyway I fronted up to this mob, did my medical and passed and was told I would be called up in about a week. The chap doing this was a fairly arrogant little corporal, who clearly thought he was "J.C," but you should have seen his face, when I told him I had volunteered my services to the RAAF, and there was no way I was going into the army! I never heard from the army again.

18th July 1942 — My RAAF Training Begins!

On the above date I reported, with 250 other new recruits to No.4 Initial Training School at Mount Breckan. Straight away my drumming abilities stood me in good stead when I was quickly made a member of the units dance band. This was great because it got me out of all sorts of other military bits of nonsense, and it also helped me in another very important way, for after six weeks of this three months course I had to front up to the category selection board, who would decide what my future training would be, e.g. pilot, navigator, bomb aimer, wireless operator / air gunner or a rear gunner. Like most of the members of this course I really only wanted to become a pilot, so you can imagine my sheer delight, when the leader of the band took me aside about a week before this interview and said, 'Blanchard, don't worry about the interview next week, all members of the band get what they want'! I thought 'you bloody beauty! I'm going to be given the chance to become a pilot'! I did my elementary flying training on Tiger Moths at No.11 Elementary Training School, Benalla, Victoria and passed with an average assessment, though sadly with no opportunity for drumming. I then went on to No. 7 service Flying Training School d' Deniliquin, New South Wales where I did my training on Wirraways, once again passed with an average assessment, won my pilots wings, was promoted to the grand rank of Sergeant, and still no drumming.   My postings then took me back to No.4 Embarkation Depot at Scotch College, Torrens Park, South Australia, then No.2 Embarkation Depot, Bradfield Park, Sydney, New South Wales. I was only there for six days, and the last night of my stay was very interesting, for the WAAF's put on a dinner dance for all these bold blokes who were about to head off to the much more dangerous areas of WWII.

I had a dance with a very attractive WAF Corporal this evening, and during the course of this dance I asked her what her function was in the Air Force, and she told me she was a radar operator. Now, in 1943, radar in Australia was a very mystic subject, and her comment made me very interested, so I asked her to tell me a bit more about it. She then went on to tell me about tracking on aircraft in South Western, New South Wales one night in April before finally losing contact with it. It took a tremendous amount of self control to stop me from bursting out laughing for I then told her that in all probability she had most likely been tracking me! On April the 4th 1943 I had to do a solo night flying exercise from Deniliquin to Echuca on the River Murray, a distance of about 45 statute miles, then return to base. It was a beautiful night, millions of stars, no moon, no turbulence and a very satisfactory arrival at my destination, with a very cocky pilot at the controls. In fact I was so cocky I did some aerobatics, and then headed for home and a well earned sleep. After about 20 minutes I could see no sign of Deniliquin so come to the conclusion I must have a head wind, and flew on for another five minutes. Still no base! I then went into the standard search pattern, flying 5 minutes east, 5 minutes south, 10 minutes west, 10 minutes north, and so on, expanding the pattern until I saw the lights of Deniliquin, Aha!! I had made it! Unfortunately as I got closer I realised that it wasn't base at all, and I had no idea where I was, but that I was at least in Australian territory! At this stage my fuel was starting to get a bit low, so I had to make a decision, bail out, or make a forced landing. I decided on the latter, and in a Wirraway aircraft a forced landing at night had to be done with the undercarriage retracted, for if you didn't, and you survived, you were scrubbed for being extremely stupid. I went into landing pattern, climbed to 4,000 feet, dropped flare No.1, descended to 1,000 feet and dropped flare No.2. The first flare had by this time unfortunately started a fire on the ground which was generating lots of smoke and as I turned onto my final approach and put on the landing light it was as though I was flying into a London Pea Soup Fog! As I was about to switch off the light I saw a huge gum tree flash past my port wingtip, so I knew I was pretty close to the ground, turned off the light, and went into the one landing drill for an emergency landing on instruments. When the altimeter read zero, I shut down the engine, eased back on the stick and did a very smooth belly landing. About 50 yards after this gently touchdown I ran into a wire fence, which brought me to a very sudden stop. Because the gear was retracted, the undercarriage warning horn was blaring quite loudly, so I got out of the cockpit, opened the small cover on the starboard side of the fuselage, shut off the master switch to enjoy a few minutes at least, of peace and quiet. The aircraft was pretty badly damaged, but the only injury I got was when

I scratched my finger on the horn position hinge spring. I had quite an audience for this time of day, and they were most solicitous, and I found out that I had landed at White Cliffs, Bendigo, Victoria, about 96 miles from where I should have been. There was a very large army tank training unit here, and one of the Sergeants took me in hand, looked after me very well for about three days, while the air force people came and dismantled the bird, packed it on the back of a huge truck, along with its pilot, then drove back to Deniliquin.On my return to base I was interviewed by the C/O, Grp/Cpt. J. Waters and had my log book endorsed, 'Forced landing, inexperience, faulty night navigation'! It never came out that I had neglected to lower the gear for resetting course for base, and this lapse could put the magnetic compass out of accuracy by up to 60 degrees or more.

The gorgeous WAAF Corporal thought this was a remarkable story and that I was a very, very lucky lad to have survived, we both chuckled over this for some time. It was now that the war started to feel much closer to me. For I boarded the troopship 'Mount Vermont' in Sydney Harbour the next day and we set sail about mid afternoon. Just after we set sail I remember all the people alongside the harbour bridge waving us farewell and shouting 'good luck'!

Our voyage was to San Francisco via Auckland New Zealand, where we were given about 12 hours shore leave. Our first view of the U.S.A was about five days later with the beautiful Golden Gate Bridge shining in the sunlight. On arrival the Americans treated us as though we had been conscripted, and the difference between their aircrew and ours was that all American pilots automatically became officers, and as we were not officers we were considered rubbish. We were not allowed to go ashore straight away but next morning we had to scale down a rope net with all our gear and taken by barge to Oakland. From here myself and some 600 other aircrew began a train journey across the United States. The carriages were very comfortable, and our attendant, a black American, was a very nice chap, who treated us very well indeed.

One of my pastimes during the trip was to measure our trains speed by timing the mile posts as they went by, it was usually just over 100mph! We stopped in Chicago at around 2 o'clock in the morning and whilst stretching our legs came across a black bloke with a tray of all sorts of goodies around his neck, a few purchases and a stroll later we were off again. My view of New York as we went through was of a station five floors below sea level, I recall it as a miserable scene. My stopping point was Camp Miles Standish, about halfway between New York and Boston. This was an American Training

Camp and it was here that I was first introduced to the US Juke Box, a huge machine holding about fifty 12 inch records by, Duke Ellington, Count Basie, Benny Goodman, Artie Show, Tommy Dorsey, Jimmy Lunceford and a host of others, I LOVED IT!!

I had the surname of some family relations in New Haven, Connecticut and I went to spend three days leave with them and we had a great time. I was approaching the front gate of Camp Miles Standish at the end of my leave as a large group of Aussies were coming out the other way. As soon as they saw me, one of them said, 'we're all shipping out in three days, it might be a good idea to do an 1800 turn and go back to where you've been!' I did not need telling twice and headed off again for another enjoyable three days.

At the end of this time, on my return to camp I heard that we were entraining in one hours time and so I hastily packed my gear and made it to parade on time. The Australian Officer there was very angry with us, for out of 600 odd in our contingent, about 99% had gone A.W.A.L. He duly informed us that on arrival at our destination we would all be charged. Now, we all figured that our destination would be the UK, and if so then the Brits would be far too busy to worry about charging us delinquents. We were correct on both counts and we never heard another thing about it. Our train took us to New York where we boarded the Ocean Liner Queen Elizabeth making our way to our allotted cabins. When my group reached the aforementioned cabin, we found nine bunks and a paliasse on the floor, guess who got the floor? Still, I wasn't bothered and in fact was very comfortable during our voyage. When I rose from my slumbers next morning we were well and truly at sea and it took me almost an hour to find the other ranks mess. We got two meals a day, as I believe there were about 15,000 Government sponsored passengers on this crossing, with the America GI's being allocated a six by three feet space in all corridors to be shared by all GI's.

The first two nights at sea were spent listening to live jazz in one of the huge reception areas, played by all sorts of muso's with top quality all round. After the second night the authorities banned this function because it got too many people in the one spot at the one time, and if we had been torpedoed the loss of life would have been enormous. The Queen Elizabeth got along at about 32 knots, and used to change course about every 15 seconds, to avoid the prevalent U-Boats that were haunting the Atlantic Ocean. About half way across we had an exciting break in routine when the ships anti aircraft batteries opened fire. Fortunately this was just a practice exercise and five days later the lovely green hills of Scotland appeared on the horizon, and although it was late June, this green looked beautiful

Our transport docked at Greenock, Scotland and our 600 got on a troop train. Within 24 hours we detrained at Brighton Sussex. Very shortly after our arrival there my mate Angus Tyson, (a very good pianist in the Fats Waller style) and I were walking along the seafront, when we saw a sign which said 'out of bounds to all service personnel'. Now being Aussies, we just looked at one another, and without a word, went to investigate. We walked down a flight of stairs and came into a fairly large room with a full length bar, complete with barman, a nicely carpeted floor with about 40 to 50 tables with several very comfortable chairs to each one, a dance floor and a podium with a semi-grand piano with a full kit of drums complete with sticks and brushes. One of us said to the barman "would you mind if we played a bit of music"? His response was "no, be my guest", we had a ball, and afterwards the barman asked us if we would be interested in playing there six nights a week, for ten shillings each a night and free drinks. How could we refuse? I think we started that same night. The news got round fast and before we knew it we were a five piece band and the 'joint was jumping' every night!

My mate Angus was posted away on his advanced flying course after two weeks but we managed to recruit a good replacement and after about four weeks of great fun we were approached by the manager of "The Dome" ballroom who wanted to know if we would be interested in relieving his big band for fifteen minutes each hour. We agreed, and if you take into account the free drinks, we were being paid almost as much as the air force was paying us, for doing something we all enjoyed and TAX FREE!

Down to the serious stuff!

However, on the 14th September it was 'down to brass tacks'!! I was posted to No. 6 Pilots Advanced Flying Unit at Little Rissington, and on the 28th September 1943 I had my first lesson in advanced flying, I must say, I could not have had a better birthday present! This course lasted four months, and was very advanced indeed. Not long after I started the training I figured that if I wanted to give myself a sporting chance of surviving this tremendous piece of human nonsense, then I must devote all my energies to flying. My drum sticks and brushes were put away, and never again used professionally.

My first six and a half weeks were spent flying with type experience, and cross country exercises, a lot of which was done with two Kiwi pilots, Flt/Sgt Madsen and F/O Blackwell. I did a low level cross country with the latter and when I went down to the Aussie low level of 150 feet he went right off his block and very brusquely said "TAKING OVER" and down we went to ground level! I'm sure he did some grass cutting during this display, it was most intriguing! The next twelve days were spent on the B.A.T. flight where for about an hour before flying one had to put on glasses with very dark blue lenses, and all cockpit windows were covered with dark yellow screens. This meant that all the pupil pilot could see were the luminous instruments, and he did everything from start up to shutdown, with of course direction guidance from his instructor. It was first class training which totalled 20 hours flying. After another 18 days day flying, I went onto the night flying training, and after 4 hours 10 minutes dual, I did 35 minutes with F/S Madsen and he was so impressed with my standard that he apologised for not being able to give me an above average assessment, The night flying system in England made our Australian one look as though it was still in the Bleriot days, for in Aussie all we had were six flares in a straight line with one at the end to make up an L shape, and a ground operator to give you a green light if it was OK to go or a red light to hold. The UK system was called DREM, it was magnificent, with a ring of white lights on a two mile radius of the aerodromes centre, with lead lights to the runway in use, with their lights only visible if you were flying into wind. There were also lead in lights from the perimeter, lights to the runway in use, along with green and red lights at the end of the strip to indicate your correct level of approach. For me it made night flying so much easier.

Every airfield in the UK during WWII had a red flashing beacon which spelt out two more code letters about every half minute, and these were changed every 24 hour, they were known as PUNDIT. In the UK there were four other beacons called OCCULTS which flashed a single Morse code letter about every minute, I think these changed monthly. There were quite a few other PUNDITS' around the UK which were slotted in dangerous country to entrap the enemy. We were given the means to avoid being fooled by these spurious beacons but sadly I can't recall what it was. It is really quite remarkable when I think of it now, for in those days, air traffic control was an unheard of term, and the amount of traffic flying round the UK was enormous though we were only aware of the merest inkling of it at the time.

My night flying near miss must have taught me a few valuable lessons because my night flying instructor told me at close of play how impressed he was, and that if he had any say in the matter I would get an "above average assessment" but for my strife once again when one morning myself and a couple of other diggers slept in. When we reported late to the flight centre we were hauled over the coals by Flt/Lt W. McRobbie. He really went to town, and apparently I was smiling during his rant, he went right off and I had the biggest strip torn off me to date!! When I sent my Christmas cards for 1943 I sent one to Lord and Lady Bledisloe, who had been Governor

General of New Zealand. I had met them both whilst at an afternoon tea and dance at Government House, Wellington, New Zealand in 1939. I received a very nice card back from them, and because it was open for all to see, word soon got around that apparently, I was well connected. McRobbie treated me with kid gloves for the rest of my stay at Little Rissington but I was keen to be involved in the obviously forthcoming invasion of Europe and applied to become a glider pilot, my application was ignored.

Even the seagulls say caaark!

When my posting came, it was to No.1 Staff pilots Training Unit at Cark in Cartmel, Lancashire, and I was brassed off at the idea, not least of all because I would be flying the MKI Avro Anson which would be the most basic aircraft I had flown to date, apart from the old Tiger Moth, which was exceptional. Things were pretty quiet at Cark during my time there with the exception of a tragic mid air collision between two Ansons near the Mull of Galloway which killed a pal of mine off the same course as me. He had taken me under his wing as I was so far from home, I was greatly saddened. There were several Polish Pilots on our course, and one of these was Sergeant Shlitzinger, and there are no prizes for guessing what everybody (including the WAFFs) called him. He had a very interesting experience on one of his early solo cross country flights, for the weather was decidedly nasty, but he successfully completed the trip and made a very rough, bumpy and damaging landing following what he believed to be a good approach. He was very upset by this, and even more upset when he discovered that he had

Ross with Anson – RAF Cark

not landed at RAF Cark, but actually in the railway yards at Lancaster!! He copped a huge amount of teasing but I'm sure he only understood half of it as he always had a broad smile on his face. A great coincidence springs to mind here, all my course numbers in Australia were 30 and I was part of

No.30 course at Cark too!

I join the staff at RAF Millom in Cumberland

I left Cark on the 7th March 1944 with another average assessment to my credit and was posted to RAF Millom No.2 Observer Advanced Flying Unit. I was no longer a pupil I was a member of "The Staff"! What a huge difference this made, plus the fact that I was now engaged in some positive activities. I was not at this station for long but I have fond memories of it. I had been having serious problems with my mail because all overseas mail was sent to a unit in London and transferred from there. I was not receiving any letters at all until suddenly I was deluged with mail because all my mail had been sent in error to No.6

Swimming – Haverigg beach

A.F.U. instead of No.6 (P) A.F.U. Sadly, one of these letters was from a pal in the Australian Navy, to tell me that a lass I was rather keen on, had been taken very ill with Scarlet Fever. I had just read this and was walking back to my quarters when I was pulled up for not saluting the station C/O, these things happen. On the plus side, I became good pals with the WAAF from the units, parachute section, her name was Mary Howarth and she was a beauty! We used to cycle down to the beach with a host of others where we enjoyed the sunshine, and some of us took a dip in the Irish Sea!

Whilst at Millom, I remember taking off one night in pretty terrible weather for a night training exercise. We were getting nowhere with our navigators training so I put the dear old "Annie" into a climb, and somewhere between 12,000 and 15,000 feet we broke clear of the cloud layer and awful weather.

Suddenly, there we were looking at all the stars and planets, crystal clear with no moon, and our trainee navigator's blood well and truly pumping! He had a ball!! When we got back on the ground at Millom our staff wireless operator said that he had been listening to a commercial radio station in New York with excellent reception. When I told him what height we had been at he almost wet his pants! Our flying roster at Millom was two weeks day / two weeks night flying and at any time if there was cloud cover on Black Combe, day flying was cancelled, but of course at night time this was not apparent, and we flew in all sorts of very nasty weather. I can recall one night in particular when towards the end of the first turbulent, training flight I was absolutely bushed, and it beats me to this day, how I got the bird down in one piece. At the second briefing on this night the Operations Officer asked if there were any pilots who would prefer to give it a miss. I was the only starter, and was excused with good grace. I think I was in the cot by 12.30am, and did not surface until about 10.00 hrs that day, which gave me about 10 minutes to get down to the next briefing. It was the only occasion that I had to do this so it got tucked away as a learning experience! Whilst at Millom I applied for a commission, and went down to the Midlands for my interview. I was successful and I became a Pilot Officer on the 24th July 1944 and one week later my posting came through.

Boomerang!

Sat in navigators position airborne over Irish Sea

I was posted back to Cark in Cartmel as a Staff Pilot Instructor! To be honest I didn't really enjoy being at Cark but I had a good pal there who was another Aussie. I can't remember his name but he was from somewhere north of Brisbane, Queensland. Anyway, there I was, sat keeping an eye on rookie staff pilots and making the most of it. I remember as a feature of WWII night flying, that at each, pre flight briefing, every pilot was given an altitude to fly at in the event of an air raid warning, and he had to circle the nearest 'PUNDIT' at that level. Now, these were only 200 feet apart, and as a result, every pilot and crew prayed very hard that every altimeter was set at the same barometric setting! At one stage I came to the conclusion that my name must have been left off the Duty Officer tasks list. This misconception was dispelled with after a long period of being detailed no duties, I found myself on duty on Christmas day 1944, it was then that the penny dropped! During this second stint at Cark I had to undertake a night training flight with a trainee squadron leader who had joined the RAF in 1937, and had not done any night flying since his early training days. We took off into the usual British night, rain, St Elmo's fire and turbulence which did nothing to bolster the Sq/Ldr's confidence! Anyway, very soon into the flight the dear old Sq/Ldr went into a steep left hand turn with a frightening loss of altitude as a result. He froze at the controls despite my comments and I was forced to take over control of the aircraft. It took all of my concentration to get back to straight and level flying, but whilst I was checking our position, I got the horrible feeling that we were once again back in a left hand steep turn, I was horrified to find us on checking, that we were in fact in a tight RIGHT hand turn! Oh dear! Back to base and glad of it! As you will have gathered, some flights remain in ones memory.

At some point in February 1945 I flew a cross country exercise right up into the hills of Scotland, with a full moon, no cloud and the ground brilliant white under a covering of snow, it was magnificent! A short time later I met up with a Lancashire lass, let us call her Miss X, we would scoot off together to all sorts of places for weekends away when I was on leave. Finally, she came to me with the news that she was expecting, so I did the so called "decent thing" and married her. Surprisingly for me, two weeks after the event she decided that, no she was not expecting and I was left to accept the embarrassing fact that I had been 'conned'!

I took my last flight with the air force on the 26th July 1945 and received my next posting very soon afterwards.

Boomerang!

My next posting was back to RAF Millom! No longer a flying unit but now No.14 Aircrew Holding Unit. The station was full of Aussies like me who were waiting to be shipped home. I was back at Millom for about two and a half months during which time I did a month's course for aircrew officers down in Hereford and a two week air sea rescue course at Blackpool after which I became Millom's A.S.R Officer.

At the end of my stay at Millom, and after three weeks in Brighton, I boarded the H.M.T. AQUITANIA for a very pleasant cruise home to Adelaide, via Freetown, Sierra Leone, and Cape Town. I was given a shore pass, and with my good mate F/O John Bails DFC in tow, set off to see the sights. We met up with a mother and daughter who very kindly put us up for the night in their home, all above board, I can assure you! And set off back next morning to re-board our boat. We managed to thumb a lift off a couple of lasses but when we got to the dock the Aquitania was just putting out to sea!! We were extremely lucky for there was an escort about to go out to the ship and on our request we were given a free ride, and climbed up a scramble net to the many cheers and catcalls of our fellow passengers. I disembarked at Sydney and arrived home by troop train on the 28th November 1945. My family were very relieved to have me back in one piece! There were many renewal gatherings with old school mates, and it was here that I learnt that out of our crowd of seven lads, only one had not come back. His name was Bruce Davies, and he was killed on a heavy bomber training flight before he even began operational duties. In March 1946 I had a talk with my Dad about a photographic exhibition I saw in London and which preyed upon my mind.

The exhibition illustrated the liberation of some of the German concentration camps. I had seen this exhibition in April 1945 and had spent about an hour trying to take it all in. It was truly horrific and it took all the willpower I had not to cry. I have only ever seen about 10% of the pictures I saw there ever displayed to the public again. I was quite appalled when my father told me that the Germans should be forgiven and our paths became quite divergent after that. I had applied for a post with Australian National Airways but the course I was to go on was cancelled, I had put in some hard work in anticipation too. Anyway, following a successful interview with Mr J.P. Rayland, the operations manager for Trans Australia Airlines, in July 1946, I was engaged as a trainee first officer with effect from the 9th September 1946 on No.3 course at Point Cook, Victoria, the course was six weeks long. I completed the course OK, did my navigators studies by correspondence course, and after a further eleven months flying, I was a fully fledged F/O. In October 1947 I was posted to Adelaide as a first officer with T.A.A. and did my first flight on Saturday the 1st November 1947. This was the inaugural flight to Darwin, via Mount Eba, Oodnadatta, Alice Springs Tennant Creek, Daly Waters and Katherine. A two pilot crew, one hostess, no VHF radio, no cockpit loudspeakers, and very little gear — we were very rarely given the OK to take the controls. Once the routine started I was averaging 75 to 80 hours a month.

I remember a couple of incidents from these days, and on both occasions the skipper was Eric Kneig. Once, after leaving Alice Springs, and finishing our airborne lunch, cruising on towards Tennants Creek I was suddenly aroused by an urgent request for a position report. I looked across and there was Eric, also sound asleep! I replied and all was well.

The second thing was during a charter flight to pick up 21 immigrants from Alice Springs. After a couple of hours I had to answer the call of nature and went to the little boy's room. Shortly after closing the door we encountered a very severe bout of turbulence during which there was a tremendous crashing in the gallery area and it rained heavily in the loo! When I returned to the cockpit it was obvious that the "turbulence" was of human instigation, as Eric was laughing his head off! In 1950 the R.A.A.F. had three de Havilland Mosquitoes based in Alice Springs doing a very comprehensive photographic survey, and being in the Air Force Reserve, I was given 2 hours and 40 minutes in one of these beautiful birds. I had a ball!! In 1951, after three attempts I passed my command training and was posted back to Adelaide, flying more or less the same roster but with many more modern aids, VHF etc.

I actually began my command training with Captain Harry Locke, D.SO, DFC who had taken part in the dambuster raids, he was a great bloke and taught me a lot. Sometime in 1952 my roster changed and I had about a 36 hour stopover period in Alice Springs. It was the time when the John Flynn memorial church was being built and I had met John Flynn when I was a small boy. At a loose end I volunteered my services as a builder's labourer to his number two, the Rev Fred McKay who insisted on paying me for my efforts. I accepted but made amends by leaving most of it behind the bar of the Alice Springs Hotel. Every time I visit and see that church I get a good feeling knowing that I helped to build it. Shortly after this I came close to getting the sack after raising concerns about pilots exceeding the 8 hour flight limitation. This matter really worried me, but resulted in a hell of a mess which could have been sorted out without all the unpleasantness it incurred had a little common sense been employed. It resulted in a good deal of disruption and me being 'sent to Coventry' but I strongly believed it was a safety issue and stuck to my guns. In the end I was told by a senior staff member that no action would be taken against me, and asked if I wanted the reports I had submitted, returned to me, I declined the offer. I told him that my reports were addressed to the Melbourne Senior Route Captain and they were now his property!

I remember one DC3 night flight from Darwin to Alice Springs in the wet season, with John Dawe as first officer. The severe turbulence began almost immediately, and it was so bad that I could only hand fly for about five minutes, with the aircraft suddenly going up at about 4,000 feet per minute, indicated airspeed about 170 knots, gear down, flaps down, no power on, then bang!, down at the same rate, about 90 knots, gear up, flaps up, full power and very savage continuous turbulence, which was so bad that it gave you eyeball bounce. This is when the body is vibrating, but the eyeballs are vibrating at a different rate, very difficult to see clearly when this occurs, it was incredible. John could also only manage about five minutes, but between us we made it. All the passengers and our hostess were sick, and it was an awful night but after a while things improved dramatically. I think of all the first officers I flew with over the years, John Dawe would have to rank among the best, and I think that, had it been someone else that night I would not be here telling this story.

In July 1958 I started my Convair 240 training, a magnificent aircraft

Much bigger than the Avro Anson!
Ross shown here at Tennant Creek Northern Territory Australia, 1963

powered by two Pratt and Whitney R2800 engines that simply growled! 40 passengers, two pilots, two hostesses, pressurised and air conditioned. I flew these lovely birds for twelve months and was then endorsed on Fokker Friendships, my first turbine powered experience and my first experience of an aircraft with "upper wing" configuration. In October 1959 I was navigator from Amsterdam to Melbourne in TAA's first MKII Fokker Friendship, a great flight via Rome, Athens, Beirut, Bahrain, Karachi, New Delhi, Calcutta, Bangkok, Saigon, Labuan, Zamboanga, Davao, Sorong, Darwin and Alice Springs. My most vivid memory is of seeing the Himalayas stretched out below us, fantastic! I carried out my last flight with T.A.a. 25/27th September 1967 due to a medical problem which no doctors seemed able to remedy, and when my sick leave ran out I retired on the 7th January 1968 after 21 years and four months. My log book showed a total of 16,127 hours 35 minutes of which 15,209 hours 45 minutes were flown with TAA, which gave me an annual average rate of 713 hours.

After leaving the airline my then wife and I went into the retail business with another couple. We built and ran seven shops in Blackwood. However, my wife's shop packed up, our marriage failed and I was out on a limb once more. I then worked in the Australian stock market for a while during the Poseidon gold boom but it was not for me and following some unpleasantness I left to take care of a farm South East of Adelaide for my stock market boss, Bob Pentelow. It was a pretty basic set up with small living accommodation, light motor bike and truck but it was OK. I soon got settled in and got some music going on my 'reel to reel' tape player, spent my days riding the fences, checking stock etc. Then one day I saw a light aircraft flying out of a nearby property. I discovered that an aero club was being set up and made myself known to those involved.

One of the new committee members was a bloke called Dr Jim Richards who took a keen interest in my retirement from flying due to my medical problem. He told me that he believed he could operate on me and fix my problem and in fact, this is what he did! Jim then told me he was setting up

Ross at Ayres Rock 1976

an air freight business and asked would I consider being his chief pilot? Of course I said yes! With medical and all formalities completed I became Chief Pilot for Meningie Air Services! I left the farm with no hard feelings and it was great to be back in the saddle once more, but as often as I flew, and no matter how much income we produced the Doc had the bad habit of spending more than came in.

After 18 months M.A.S. had to close down. I received the odd offer but decided to go it alone and set up Blanchard Air Charter. This was one of the best decisions I have ever made. There were many interesting flights in over 50 different types of Aircraft, ranging from Cessna 172's on whale spotting trips to freight runs in a Lear Jet. I remember one flight in the Lear, climbing to 50,000 feet just before sunrise when the curvature of the earth was clearly visible. I undertook many bush flights and one of my stopovers was Ernabella, an Aboriginal settlement, and I used to join up with Barry Jeromsen, a school master there and run with him out to the airport and back (about 16KMs). We were running one day when we saw an Aborigine sniffing a can of petrol, he looked about 40 years old to me, it turned out he was one of Barry's students — a nasty thing and still a problem today in Australia. Barry ran 2 hours and 49 minutes for the marathon in later years and I set a state Male 60 record at 3 hours 1 min 27 seconds, great to look back on! In 1988 I contracted Viral Encephalitis which did some very nasty things to me and my wife Jenny was forced to shut down my Air Charter Business. It took me about 5 years to get even close to back to normal.

Swan Song

My No.1 Swan Song was in October 1993 when I hired a Piper Lance to take us touring some of my old friends and haunts. The owner very kindly removed the rear seats so that we could take along our bicycles for ground transport and our luggage for the trip. We visited Benalla, where I had done my initial flight training, Deniliquin, from where I flew my navigational disaster! met some old TAA pals in Cowra NSW then on to Lismore to meet more old friends. From there we began quite a tour finishing up in the North Flinders Ranges for three days before flying home. With all latitudes and longitudes logged carefully into my G.P.S. I am pleased to say that all destinations appeared on time!! 1994 was a great year, with an overseas trip to the UK via Honolulu, Vancouver and Alaska, with of course, that very special meeting with you all at Millom.

Swan Song No.2 was June 1995 when my wife Jenny and I set off once again on our travels, same gear, same aircraft but different route. This time we flew a total of 35 hours via Ceduna SA, Port Augusta, Ayers rock Giles Meteorological Station in central Australia, on to Newman W.A. then up to Broome where we spent three days. From Broome we went coastal all the way home via Hedland, Geraldton, Jandakot, Albany, Esperance and Port Lincoln, a great holiday. On November 11th I was taken for two flights, one in a replica of Sir Charles Kingford Smiths Fokker, and the second in a Wirraway, happy memories! In December 1995 I was appointed "Check

Captain" in James Morrison's (the world renowned Jazz musician) Navajo Chieftan for an overnight stop at Williams Creek SA. It was a great night with James playing some great stuff and his brother John playing drums on all sorts of pots and pans, loads of guests, some of whom had travelled over 100K to fire up the party.

Swan Song No.3 was a flight up to Broome where Jenny was running a convention, we hired a Cessna 172, flew coastal, a great trip.

Swan Song No.4, Boxing Day 1996 we flew to the Australian Jazz convention in Bathurst NSW, again we hired the Cessna 172 and had a great time.

Ross & author 1994

Well, can't spin the Swansongs out forever! I had my last legal flight in James Morrison's Navajo Chieftan on the 5th February 1998 with his brother John as skipper, and end of my flying days after nearly 56 years!

A final summary:

1942-46 .... **R.A.A.F, The most exciting & by far the most dangerous years**

1946-1968 .... **T.A.A. The most educational years**

1970-73 .... **Private flying, the most expensive years!**

1973-1988 .... **M.A.S. and B.A.C, The most interesting years**

1988-1998 .... **Private flying, once again the most expensive years but including the magnificent 'Swan Song' flights!**

Keeping in mind the summary of man's 95 years of heavier than air flight, 1903 – 1998 it is satisfying to note that I have been involved for very nearly 56 of those years!

Ross Blanchard 2004

Mr R.A. Croxall – Cark 1943

"I arrived at RAF Cark on the 2nd July 1943 having been posted in as a Staff Wireless Operator from the radio school at RAF Madley. Having examined my log book I see that I was involved in a forced landing at RAF Millom on the 15th July after problems with our MK1 Avro Anson. Our pilot that day was Pilot/SGT Colling and fortunately we escaped the incident without injury.

During my time at the station I flew exclusively in Ansons and my pilots were SGT Roberts, F/O Clarkson, P/O Bowen, P/O McKillingon, SGT Wright and SGT Tennyson. The aircraft I flew in whilst there were J2, C3, J3, M3, N1, M1 K2, C2, L4 and K1. Our job was to take part in various navigational exercises and during my stay at the unit I clocked up 37 hours and 45 minutes; 28 hours 50 minutes daytime flying and 8 hours 55 minutes night flying. Our Senior Instructor was F/O S B Durrant and my lasting memory of Cark is that of a very happy station.

At the end of December 1943 I was posted to RAF Bishops Count in Northern Ireland as an instructor to the trainee wireless operators there. Having completed a spell there I teamed up with an old school friend who was now a pilot. The pair of us passed through an Operational Training Unit en route to 'Ops', with first of all 199 Squadron and latterly with 171 Squadron, carrying out special duties in support of Bomber Command. Unfortunately, on our fourth 'op' we crashed on take-off, with my old school pal receiving the blame and being posted out as a consequence.

I finally completed my operational tour on the 13th March 1945 and the rest, as they say, is history. For the record, the pilot who replaced my pal was S/L Sturrock, a New Zealander.

I hope my memories of Cark are of use, I do recall fondly a very cosy pub in the village where I spent some happy hours!"

Mr R A Croxall – 2011

Alfred Wise Dudley - *The Uniform Years 1940 - 1946*

Prologue to my attempt to produce some sort of record of my wartime years, this, some 65 years after the actual events took place, but with, hopefully, enough memory recall left to establish a reasonably accurate chronicle of my life in uniform; "The Uniform Years".

I write this in somewhat unusual circumstances, as this is December 26th 2005, and finds me on holiday in Fuerteventura enjoying a very unusual Christmas and New Year, quite unlike any I have experienced before, with warm sunny days, although I have no doubt that by the time I get around to finishing this I will be back in the U.K. with the usual mix of long, dark, wet, cold days.

Strictly speaking, I suppose with regard to the wearing of uniform I should start with my Home Guard time or Local Defence Volunteers (L.D.V.) as it was first known. This was formed post Dunkirk, in May 1940, and open to everyone to volunteer above the age of 17. A bit of a "bits and pieces" arrangement to start with, but did become more professional as time went on with the issue of uniforms and rifles, and now looking like a sort of army. Not, I think, that it would have been much of a match for any invading forces dropping out of the sky, with a maximum of 5 rounds of ammunition available per man. We had our share of "Dads Army" characters too, they were all there; if it hadn't been about such a serious business, it would have been a laugh a minute, however, I suppose it did achieve a degree of propaganda and confused the enemies thinking, it certainly confused a lot of people here!

The really serious uniform time started rather later, and my first attempt to be of assistance in the conflict was early August 1940, a week after my 18th birthday. I made my way to the joint recruiting office in Manchester to volunteer for flying duties, but after a couple of interviews and some form filling, I was informed that I could not be accepted for aircrew training, as my educational qualifications were not of the required high standard, (I had of course left school at the age of 14). However, I was told I could join the R.A.F as a general duties entrant, this offer I rejected and said I would go next door and join the Navy, not that I had any intention of doing this, there was too much cold water involved there!

However, my next attempt in April 1941 did meet with rather more success, as the reality of the situation had finally become recognised, in as much as losses in personnel were overtaking new entrants coming in, and the strict educational requirements were having to be relaxed to further a push for higher numbers to be brought into the system.

The powers that be therefore agreed that I could be finally accepted for aircrew training, and could be actually allowed to get into one of their aeroplanes! So it was off to Padgate for the aircrew selection board and medicals.

The medical examination was giving me some cause for concern at this time, as I had rheumatic fever as a child and was aware that I had a heart murmur as is usual post this illness, and I also knew that this would have precluded me from aircrew duties, so I omitted to mention this on the form I was given to complete listing childhood illnesses, and hoped for the best. Fortunately a lot of the doctors who were doing the medicals were older retired practitioners who had been brought in to fill the gaps, and were not over efficient, and the sheer numbers going through meant that things were a little rushed. My murmur was not picked up, even after the preliminary checks of

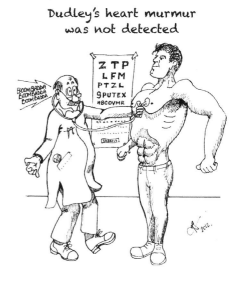

Dudley's heart murmur was not detected

blowing up a column of mercury and holding it for one minute and the quick whizz round in a chair and then standing on one leg, and various other things to be completed pre- medical.

More interviews followed, the whole process taking two full days, and then, finally accepted as a trainee WOP/AG (wireless operator/machine gunner), sworn in, accepted the "Kings Shilling", and then designated the service number 1049069; and from that point on I was indeed just a number.

After this it was back to my civilian status and also the Home Guard on deferred service to wait until my number came up in the queue for places in the training schools. This finally arrived on September 19th 1941, and it was of to Padgate again for kitting out, and then to Blackpool for the start of training proper.

I spent 4 months at Blackpool doing all the usual training stuff, drills etc. plus a round of inoculations, anti typhoid, typhus, malaria etc. all in anticipation of overseas postings, pretty vicious stuff it was too, knocked me out for nearly a week, and for a couple of days I didn't know whether my arm belonged to me or not, these all to be topped up at a later date; I made a mental note of avoiding the next time, thinking there had to be a way of giving it all a miss, but more of that later. The most focus of the training was on learning and using the Morse code, this was relentless and aimed at getting up to speed by a certain time. There were various venues for this, the best of which was the Winter Gardens, and the worst was the disused Tram sheds, which was where I unfortunately was allocated to, they were cold, flag floors, no heating, as the weather got colder necessitated in the wearing of overcoats and gloves, sat on long tables  with a pair of earphones clamped on over a cap, this for 2x2 hour sessions every day, an a occasionally 3 periods. Really it was mass learning by saturation, with a test every 2 weeks, and the speed being increased up to a maximum of 12 words per minute for passing out, there was only one second chance for a failed test, and if failed again it was a case of cease training, commonly known as CXd. Understandably this pressure of continuous Morse in the headset did affect a few people, and resulted in a degree of temporary insanity; with 3 or 4 weeks in a psychiatric unit,(Feldmans Arcade had been adapted for this purpose), they recovered quite quickly but were never allowed to return to the business of "Morse" in any shape or form.

Training apart, the things that most remain in my mind about Blackpool, were, on the plus side, the wonderful efficiency of bath parades, these twice a week at Derby Baths, (long gone now of course) with thousands going through every day, and if the shower was taken quickly there was time for a few lengths in the main pool; it was all timed extremely well, with my squad allocated 5.15pm every Tuesday and Friday. The local hospitality was much in evidence too, and I remember particularly the cheap rides on the sea front Trams, this was a maximum of one penny if in uniform, regardless of the distance travelled, and one could ride from Squires gate to Fleetwood for this.

On the downside was my billet, it must have been one of the worst in Blackpool, 28 of us in there, the food was awful, never properly cooked, and e.g. the same pudding every day of the week, and only a change on Sunday when it was rice. The landlady employed 3 or 4 young Jewish girls (refugees), and paid them a pittance, and she was regularly seen going out by taxi in the evenings dripping in gold jewellery. There was a resident Corporal, who we had to address complaints to, but it didn't make any difference, I have always believed that he was getting a good pay off every week. Most of those Blackpool Landladies did a really good job, and treated twi-SR boarders like their own sons, but for just a few it was an opportunity to make a lot more money than they had ever been able to make running second rate boarding houses. Afterwards I lived on many camps where cooking was on a mass produced scale, but never any as bad as my Blackpool experience, at least I was never hungry again, and didn't have to spend every penny I could spare on buying food!

Now, after acquiring the necessary speed of taking Morse, it was time to move on, and after a weeks leave, it was off down to Yatesbury in Wiltshire, this being January 1942.

A cold bleak January it was, and turned into a long winter, continuously frozen up everywhere, and lasting until mid March. Not much heating in the huts or in the cookhouse which was a large Spartan building, with seating for up to a thousand; by the time food had been collected and taken to the table there wasn't a lot of warmth left in it! However, one got used to the conditions eventually, and as well as the continuation of the process of gradually increasing Morse speeds, there were now classroom and workshop periods, learning about the technical side of radio, fault finding experience mostly, to be able to decide which valve/fuse to change if the equipment went down whilst airborne, we also had some responsibility for the general electrical systems of the aircraft.

Perhaps before I move on from the Yatesbury period, there are a couple of incidents worth mentioning, one of which was the weekly sports afternoon, when everyone was expected to participate, it was football or rugby for many, as there where a dozen or so pitches available, but as I wasn't any good at either of these, I found myself, along with a thousand or so others, taking part in a cross country run. Now if it had been nice summer weather this would have been tolerable, but it was mid winter and the ground was frozen solid, and clad only in a T-shirt and shorts and a pair of thin plimsolls, it really wasn't much fun. I remember seeing a string of racehorses being exercised as we ran over the frozen ground, alright for them though, they were covered in heavy blankets, and I thought there must be a better way of spending Wednesday afternoons than this. Sure enough the opportunity arose with a notice appearing on the notice board announcing the start of evening fencing classes, one night a week for 2 hours, and I thought that enrolling for these might just be a good investment. with not many willing to give up an evening, and so it proved to be, as when the next sports day arrived I found myself excused to attend further fencing classes. I never actually made much progress with the fencing apart from learning how to put on the equipment, and the difference between a Foil, an Epee, and a Sabre, but as it all took place in a nice warm hut it took care of my sports afternoons; there was always a way to beat the system!

The other small episode that might be worth mentioning concerns the next round of vaccinations, I didn't much fancy these, so after observing the procedure and knowing my day I prepared myself by a visit to the NAAFI store to buy a packet of plasters, armed with these I went down to the medical hut and joined the queue waiting for injections, rolled up my sleeve and stuck a plaster on my arm, I then joined the queue waiting to have pay books stamped to confirm injections given and displayed my bit of plaster, result,(pay book stamped and all quite painless, with no after affects at all!!), as I mentioned before, there was always a way.

My time at Yatesbury finally ended in April 1942,and after the end of term exams, I was finally a fully trained radio operator, and in receipt of a 50% rise in pay, still not great but welcome nevertheless, it was actually from 3 shillings per day to 4 shillings and 6 pence. (In the metric scale this would be from 15p a day to 22 p a day, difficult to make comparisons due to much changed values). Finally it was home leave for a week and then on my way to no. 10 Air Gunnery School as a staff radio operator, ground service.

When I was first informed that my posting was to Walney Island I thought that I was going overseas as I had never heard of it, but I suppose it was overseas in a way, being an island, but I was relieved to discover it only a short bus ride across the estuary from Barrow-in-Furness. The channel was up to the shipyards on the Barrow side, where the submarines being made were launched, I often stood on the bridge and watched, and wondered how many of their crews would survive the war .I remained at Walney for most of the summer of 1942, not leaving until mid August, This proved to be a very enjoyable period, as being a radio operator and working shifts, I was excused all other duties and parades, and lived in a hut designated as a signals hut", with all the other signals operators, and it was all very comfortable, We worked 12 hour shifts, alternate weeks on days and nights, with very little in the way of radio traffic, particularly '51 night, but we were required to listen to Group Control broadcasts every hour, with an occasional individual message to 10 AGS not that these were very important, I think it was just to make sure we were still awake!, The whole network, with control at Preston, covered all the west coast, and was in place as a back-up in case of landlines being destroyed by enemy action. We had one day off a week, and as it was a particularly good summer, I made a habit of getting up mid afternoon when on nights and going down to the beach for a couple of hours with a book, returning in time for an evening meal before going on "watch ", 8 to 8 were the hours. Sadly, as all good things must, it came to an end, and I found myself on my way down to London to no.7 signals school, but that is another episode.

Arrived in London, South Kensington SW7, in mid August 1942, no.7 signals school to be precise, the whole school were billeted in a block of flats, known as Albert Court Flats, and were directly opposite the Albert Hall; they had been and indeed still are, "Luxury Flats", all fittings had been stripped out of course, apart from essentials, and the lifts no longer worked; not a lot of fun when living on the 6th Floor as I was, with 2 flights of stairs to each floor, very up market after living in a hut, I think nearly everyone was surprised to find baths fitted with glass doors, some more so than others, having probably never seen a bathroom before, there were a dozen or so of us to each flat.

The course was of 14 weeks duration, and designated as a Radio Maintenance Course, and I only discovered in recent years that after passing out I had become "Aircraftman 1st class Radio Operator Mechanic", I don't remember ever noticing the increase in pay that should have gone with this sudden elevation in rank, wouldn't have been much though! Our classrooms were in the science museum, which had been stripped of all its contents for safe keeping until after the war's end; workshops were in what had been the sculpture galleries and our dining room was in the basement of the arts building. A bit of a doubtful place this for a dining area, as I remember when on one occasion a drowned rat was discovered at the bottom of one of the large tea urns, kind of puts you off tea! We paraded daily on Cromwell Road before going off to classes, P/T was in Hyde Park, quite pleasant this though, as in the early days when the weather was still warm, a swim in the Serpentine was the order of the day, and when the weather was inclement P/T periods were in the Albert Hall, suppose I can always claim to have appeared there.

As we were now in an advanced stage of training we did not have to be back in Barracks until 23.59 Hrs each evening, a privilege this for a training school, it was usually 22.30 Hrs. I was not the least familiar with the way around London, but soon found the Tube System made it possible to quickly find the way to anywhere. With very little spare cash, it was not possible to sample many of the attractions that were still available, but I did manage a visit to St. Paul's' Cathedral and to Kew Gardens plus an occasional walk along the embankment, and a few visits to speakers corner. I also remember what the best forces canteen I ever encountered was probably, it was in the basement of the Brompton Oratory, and staffed by the ladies of the church, food and drinks were excellent with occasionally cream cakes on the menu. (How did they do it?) Mid January 1943 brought to and end my stay in the capital, it was a pleasurable enough period, and now I found myself on the way to Madley in Herefordshire, to at last be introduced to a real aeroplane!

Madley did not appear to be very hospitable on arrival, it was a wartime built establishment, hurriedly put together, Nissan Huts and everywhere widely dispersed; each section seemed to be at least half a mile apart, with a long walk to the ablution site. After the long walk for a wash, it was a further long hikes to dining hall and classrooms, with a final stretch down to the flights, never being anywhere near the point of residence again all day, and it was essential to carry small kit around all the time i.e. shave and wash gear, and eating utensils. However, the course was quite enjoyable, and mainly aimed at using the radio equipment whilst airborne, at first in Dominies, a twin engine aircraft, and really quite small, but with enough space for 5 pupils, and an instructor plus pilot, virtually a flying classroom which worked very well.

The last 2 weeks were spent going solo in a single engine aircraft, Proctors, with just a pilot and then doing individual work on the radio, I found the whole process very pleasant, particularly so as flying was a completely new experience, as indeed it was for most of us, I really enjoyed flying up and down the Wye Valley. This all came to an end in early March 1943, and I was on my way to gunnery school for a course in air gunnery.

So now I was off to Mona in Anglesey to no. 3 A.G.S. again this was a somewhat dispersed establishment, with Nissan Huts for accommodation, and cold they were in that part of the year, with just a shelf running down each side of the hut, very active those shelves were too at night, with mice running up and down.

Air Gunnery practice was done from Blackburn Botha's, not a very comfortable aircraft, and extremely unpopular with most aircrew. Three pupils for each aircraft were carried, with 2 machine guns in the turret to fire 200 rounds each, we fired at a drogue towed by another aircraft, the tips of the bullets were coloured in order to establish which pupil was responsible for each hole in the drogue, they were then dropped in the dropping field, where they were then collected by W.A.A.F.'s, (Women's Auxiliary Air Force), and the holes duly counted, I sometimes think they would add a few more hits to the score if they thought someone had a poor score, I never heard of anyone actually failing the course ! In my end of term report I see that I was assessed as above average, I think some kind W.A.A.F. must have added a few to my total.

When firing was completed some of the Pilots would fly up to Blackpool to go round the tower a couple of times. One other incident occurred after a couple of weeks when we had started with the flying side of the course. I got my flying boots off the shelf in the hut, and a dozen or so little pink mice

dropped out of them, it appeared that Mr. And Mrs. Mouse had set up home there, not much fur left on the boot! So it was off down to stores to exchange them for new pair, did me a good turn actually as the ones I got were a much better style and quality than the ones I was discarding.

My time at Mona came to an end in late March 1943, and with passing out this time came promotion to the somewhat exalted rank of Sgt, and with this came a very welcome increase in pay, difficult to quantify in terms of today's wages, but it more or less doubled my then current income. With the passing out parade came the list of postings to say where I was headed off to after a weeks leave, and I found myself due to report to R.A.F. Cark, no. 1 S.P.T.U. I had no idea at the time what sort of establishment it was, or indeed where it was but I was soon to find out!!

It sounded very interesting when I found out it was close to Grange over Sands, that set the location, but I was still in the dark as to knowing what it was, but I was soon to find out on my arrival at Cark. Another course, they seemed never ending, now to be aimed at turning me into a Radio Instructor, Air Operating, it all sounded very grand and I could not imagine why I found myself earmarked for this, and can only think, in retrospect that my number had just been pulled out of a hat somewhere; I'm sure it wasn't due to any special ability on my part.

This six week spell proved to be very enjoyable as it was now late spring, with a lot of fair weather periods, not much of the time was spent in classrooms, mostly it was spent airborne without an instructor; it was really just a case of working through the syllabus whilst flying on cross country exercises. We had a second pilot, one flying whilst the other did the navigating, they were training to be navigational instructors, to fly trainee navigators around, hence the name, "Staff Pilot Training Unit". My course work consisted mainly of supplying these trainee Pilot/Navigators with enough in the way of Fixes and Bearings to enable them to plot their course.

The aircraft in use were Anson's, in which I was to spend a lot of my time during the ensuing 18 months; I found them very comfortable if a little overcrowded with 5 crew members. Nothing exceptional occurred whilst at Cark, the only thing of note that I remember was flying in formation over Carnforth one Saturday afternoon, where they were having a "Fund raising day" for the war effort.

On completion of the course I found myself on the way to Millom, designated no.2 A.F.U. that is to say" Advanced Flying Unit where the pupils were already qualified aircrew, and were there to gain further air experience.

Millom seemed to be agreeable and friendly enough on my arrival, when I found my quarters were to be a single room contained in a block, very small and sparsely furnished but nevertheless a pleasant change from living in a barrack block, it contained a bed, a small but comfortable enough chair and a small table covered with a piece of old blanket. There were no facilities for hanging clothes up, but a couple of nails in the wall took care of that. Heating consisted of just a single pipe running through the room, and I noted that there would be just enough space to park my cycle, the communal ablutions were situated at one end of the block, all very nice though, particularly so as this was the first time in my life that I had a room of my own! (I was now 20 years of age.)

On checking out the routines I found out that the mess was only a hundred yards away, and Millom itself about 3 miles distance, hence the bike was to prove very useful over the following 18 months. A private laundry service was provided through the mess, paid for through a mess bill at the end of each month, apart from clothing sheets were changed weekly, (as aircrew an extra privilege was to always have sheets) the mess always able to come up with extra rations such as eggs and poultry, much of it I suspect obtained via the black market and the farms of the Lake District. Meal times were somewhat changed, with the main meal of the day now being evening dinner, this to accommodate ever changing flight times, all of which was to maximise air time at 24 hours a day weather permitting. A light meal was served at lunchtime, with afternoon tea with sandwiches available in the anteroom for those who required them at about 4p.m. we enjoyed waitress service for evening dinner, all in all it really was very civilised.

The downside to all this of course was having to be available to fly at any time of the day or night when the weather was deemed suitable, we flew in some fairly dodgy conditions, and as Anson's were not equipped with any de-icing facilities, plus the fact that they had a ceiling of about 12,000 feet, and could not often fly above the clouds, meaning that on frosty nights we were briefed to take care when approaching high ground!

On an organisational level we were divided into 4 flights, 2 flights on days and 2 on days, we flew alternate fortnights days and nights, with one day off each week. Days off were usually spent In Barrow, with evenings in Millom when not scheduled to fly, the local pubs being the favourite venues. (Not much else to do in Millom) There was always the option of an early return to the mess when the pumps ran dry, as frequently happened in those days. Home leave came quite frequently; being aircrew we were allowed one week off in every six, normally taken as a fortnight every 3 months.

However we did not suffer anywhere near the casualty rates of Bomber Command, where life expectancy for a new crew at this time was 5 operational flights; we did however suffer occasional accidents, with the limited capabilities of the aircraft many of which had been well used before arriving at Millom, and this, coupled with the fact that servicing was somewhat minimal, did lead to some problems. It has to be said though that most accidents with fatalities occurred due to weather conditions or errors in navigation, mountains or high ground did have a nasty habit of getting in the way! We lost about a dozen aircraft with crews during my time there, plus many other accidents of a lesser degree; not that we were any different to other air training establishments, there were crashes of one sort or another every day, over 100 aircraft perished on the slopes of Snowdon during those years, 4 of our Ansons during my period found their graveyard there.

All of this apart, I really quite enjoyed my time there; between Walney, Cark, and Millom I spent about half of my service life in that SW corner of the Lake District. It is only in retrospect that I perceive many of the delights there were in spending time in that neck of the woods, one that I particularly remember is of returning from the west after night details just as dawn was breaking on summer mornings, and flying into the rising sun, and seeing from the observation dome the mountains casting their first shadows, with the sun's rays reflecting from the lakes, not that this was seen as anything special at the time, all we were thinking about then was getting back to egg, chips, and often bacon also, that would be served between night details; and if on the final flight, hoping that the next nights flying would be cancelled so that a visit to town could be arranged!

One other duty that should have been appreciated but wasn't, occurred only occasionally, twice in my case, involved changing the batteries on the mountain warning transmitters that were situated on high ground. These were heavy duty car type batteries carried in back packs designed for the purpose, certainly heavy! We were in teams of 6 and took turns in carrying them, the whole process in getting to the top and back down again took about 5 or 6 hours, I remember on one occasion having to use ice picks to gain access to the container housing the equipment. When the changing process had been completed the discharged batteries had to be carried back down the mountain side, suppose I can always claim to have climbed Scafell and Skiddaw, not so much of a climb really, as we were guided up the easy route by a local guide, it was heavy going though; there was however a bonus at the end of the day in the form of a evening meal laid on at a local hostelry, on one occasion this was the "Royal Oak Ambleside".

I was fortunate during my time at Millom not to a have been involved in any accidents of any description, even minor ones, but I did avoid (if that is the

right word) 2 accidents that led to fatalities, simply because fate decreed that I was not in the wrong place at the wrong time The first of these occurred in my early time there before we had become established with regular crews, one of my group asked me if I would mind changing with him because he had become friendly with a particular pilot, I agreed and on their first flight together the aircraft started to vibrate and finally broke up over St.Bees Head, they were all killed. The second occasion was on a weekend leave taken to be best man at a friends wedding, and when I returned from leave on the Sunday evening, I discovered that the crew that I would have been flying with had I not been on leave, had crashed in Northern Ireland, with 2 crew members killed and the others in hospital, and thus it would appear that the Gods were being extremely kind to me.

Two other small items that just might be worth mentioning, rather amusing both of them. The mess adopted a young jackdaw that had an injured wing and had difficulty flying, it quickly became at home in the dining room due to the scraps of food readily available, and also developed a taste for beer and would perch on the glasses on the bar and drink from them, as you may well imagine this behaviour was much encouraged. The problems started when it was introduced to whisky, and had great difficulty standing on one leg after a few drops of the short stuff and immediately fell over, leading to much hilarity all round, afterwards settling in a corner of an armchair, sleeping off the affects before waking up with an obvious hangover, with feathers on it's head standing to attention! Sadly it only survived for about 6 months,

" IF YOU LET ME GO I COULD 'HOWT G'NAGIVATE THE LOT OF YOU!" HIC !

being so slow on the wing I can only imagine that some predator had a bit of a feast.

The other small detail that maybe of some interest concerns the toilet facilities on the Anson's, as the aircraft was comparatively small there was no elsan available, just a funnel with a tube leading out into the slipstream for emptying one's bladder, bit crude this, I often wondered about what some honest citizen passing underneath must have thought, probably, "That's funny, I didn't think it would rain today".

My time at Millom came to a sudden end, as all good periods must, when I returned from Christmas leave in 1944 to discover that all flying had ceased, there no longer being the need for more and more crews, quite suddenly there were more trained aircrew available than were required. The war in Europe was moving toward closure and consequently demands were diminishing, so I, along with all the other flying personnel, found ourselves on the move again. I had enjoyed a comparatively comfortable 18 months, and if nothing else I did depart with 600 odd hours of flying time in my log book, and an extensive knowledge of the NW coast of Wales and the SW coast of Scotland including the "Mull of Galloway" and the "Mull of Kintyre". I departed for pastures new on the 1st of January 1945 wondering what the next 18 months would bring.

"Wing" in Bedfordshire was the next port of call, it was no. 26 O.T.U. (operational training unit), and I found myself part of a crew of 6 flying in Wellington Aircraft, generally known as "Wimpeys". The training we did was mostly cross country navigational exercises, in fact, similar to what I had been doing for the previous 18 months, but, with the greater range of the Wellington, trips now averaged 5 or 6 hours duration. At 22 years of age, I was the oldest member of the crew and also the most experienced, with more actual flying time than the other 5 added together. My job was more or less the same as my work at Millom, but rather easier as I did not have a trainee to guide through the various procedures. We did all the fringe bits and pieces of course, Dinghy Drill, Simulation High Altitude chamber etc. I do not remember anything very special about this period, apart perhaps from a couple of trips over Normandy, (The war had by this time moved into Germany) from which time my memories are of seeing all the dead livestock lying in the fields waiting for someone to come along and clear up. The only other point is that I had now reached the somewhat exalted rank of "Warrant Officer", a rank I was able to exploit to the full during the rest of the time I still had to remain in the R.A.F.

Mid April 1945 saw me on the move again, going on leave, to await instructions as to where to report next, normal procedures meant that this would be a H.C.U. (Heavy Conversion Unit) but that was not to be. My leave was constantly extended via a weekly telegram and a fortnightly pay voucher to be cashed at the post office, this went on for 3 or 4 weeks and during this time the war in Europe ended, leaving me wondering "What next", for the war in the Far East was still being pursued. However, my instructions finally arrived and I was on my way to Acaster Malbis, a place I had never heard of, but was relieved to find it was only about 5 miles outside York.

I duly arrived there in early May to find that it had been a Bomber Command airfield which had been mothballed, but was now being re-opened to accommodate all the redundant aircrew who were in limbo, all channels now being full as replacements were no longer required. All was chaotic initially with no one seeming to have much idea about what was going on, but we were being fed and watered and indeed paid, on this point perhaps I should mention that now, as a Warrant Officer, I no longer had to attend pay parade, just simply called in the accounts dept. and signed for my cash, really quite civilised. Some sort of order was eventually established, with interviewing panels set up to send individuals off in various directions and career changes. Some crews and indeed the ones from my O.T.U. course were included, were posted off to Transport Command where there was much work still to be done. Unfortunately I was now part of a headless crew, as my pilot, being Canadian, had been sent off down to Fleetwood where all the Canadians were being assembled to await transport home, as Canada no longer had any commitments, not being involved in the war in the Far East.

Thus ended my flying days. It was to be years before I would fly again, and next time, rather than being paid to fly, I had to pay to fly! Very different now from the sort of flying I had been accustomed to, now it is just a bus ride without the scenery.

It was now interview time to discover where I would be going next, returning to flying duties was not an option, there were just too many trained aircrew in the system, the choices were somewhat limited, and I finally opted for a radar mechanics course; two reasons, I thought the knowledge might be useful after the war with the possible advent of T.V. and I knew the course was down at Yatesbury where I had spent some time before, and I rather fancied another spell there with the new freedom that I could enjoy as a Warrant Officer. Now it was a matter of waiting for a vacancy on a course, this took several weeks, and I rather enjoyed what remained of my time at Acaster.

There was really nothing to do now but await for a posting to come through, and so I, along with several friends, established an almost daily routine of; a morning lie in until about 10 a.m. an early lunch in the mess, then down to York for a couple of hours on the river in a hired skiff, one of my friends was a member of Chester Rowing Club and was very enthusiastic about the river. Consequently, as a result of these sessions I became reasonably competent in the rowing skills and enjoyed those hours on the River Ouse. After an afternoon on the river it was off to Betty's Cafe for afternoon tea, and then downstairs to Betty's Bar which was downstairs in the same building, stay there until closing time or until the beer ran out, then back to the mess to occupy the bar there until about midnight with another day of waiting completed.

One episode occurred during my stay at Acaster which I feel obliged to mention, although somewhat reluctantly as I still feel it that it was a rather foolish escapade to be a part of. There had been a 21st. birthday party in the mess, (There was one almost every week) and as I was making my way back to my quarters with two of my rowing companions after rather more than a few drinks we started to speculate as to what it would be like to go out on the river in the moonlight as it was a beautiful early summer evening with a full moon.

On our way back to quarters we came across a Canadian YMCA van parked by an empty building, with keys in the ignition lock, tried them and the engine started, so it was suggested that perhaps we could borrow it and go down to York for a midnight row. That said the three of us squeezed into the seat and I volunteered to do the driving, collectively we did not have any experience but I was confident I could get us down to the river. I did know what the clutch, brake pedal. and throttle were for, but my problem was combining all these functions to work in unison, however we finally got under way, and did arrive at our destination, after a rather jerky and slow journey, with the use of only a couple of gears. We parked the van close to the boatyard by the" Ouse Bridge Inn" and made our way to the skiffs which were just tethered to the mooring pegs, and quite available. A small problem now arose, not an oar in sight, they were all locked away in a long heavily padlocked shed, so our attempt to take a moonlight cruise had to be abandoned. This proved to be fortuitous as had we actually got onto the river, we could have found ourselves in serious difficulty, it was spring and if there had been a strong ebb tide running we may well have found ourselves on the way to the Humber Basin, for these tides were difficult enough to row against even in broad daylight and stone cold sober! We re-embarked into the van, with another member of our group insisting on doing the driving, he wasn't I think as adept as myself; at least I managed to stay in the middle of the road. On the way back we picked up two airmen hitching a lift, it was now about 2am, there was no room inside so one stood on each side of the cab on the running board, but it wasn't long before we lost them. brushed off against the hedge. Shortly afterwards our journey came to an end with the van stuck in a ditch, it proved impossible to get it out, and as we were only a few hundred yards away from our destination we abandoned it and walked back.

The following morning there was much activity by the RAF police, making enquiries and obtaining a tractor to pull the van out of the ditch, they didn't make much progress with solving the crime; they were not very good and faced an impossible task with hundreds coming in each day and hundreds departing. One finally irony was that an airman was observed later that day walking around with a plaster on and his arm in a sling, it was rumoured that he claimed to have been knocked off the side of a van, but I don't think anyone believed him! My posting finally came through and I was on my way down to Yatesbury once more and quite looking forward to the career change.

Thus the beginning of July 1945 saw me settling in down in Wiltshire, nice homecoming in a way, and comfortable in the knowledge that all that cross country running was no longer a threat. I was actually in a unique situation, as the remainder of my group were all new recruits, subject of course to all the parade ground stuff and other pastimes that passed for initial training. With my new rank I could of course avoid all this and I went on to exploit my new situation to the full, classroom work and technical work in the labs was the general order of things, and I made a point of attending those but nothing else. In the classrooms I found we were on a course of mathematics, and I rather enjoyed the opportunity to extend my somewhat elementary knowledge of that subject. I also picked up a few bits of know how in the workshops, e.g., using a soldering iron for much finer work than that met with a couple of years earlier at no.7 signals school, I also learned to use a Vernier, a Micrometer, and a slide rule, skills not much in demand these days. Apart from course work my time was my own, and this I spent between my quarters (I had my own room again), the mess. and later in the day the Lansdowne Hotel down in Calne, with a break for tea in one of the cafes, which all seemed to be owned by Harris's, the well known pie merchants. All things considered it was an enjoyable period, and in retrospect I suppose my life then was equivalent to that of a college student today, only turning up in the training wing when I thought it was worthwhile, with the advantage of course that I did not have any financial obligations. This all came to an end when the war in the Far East ended, and forces requirements were again reviewed, with information starting to come through about demobilisation dates.

The radar course that I was on was a long one of 2 years duration, split into 10 week segments, I had just finished the first one and learned that I had the option of taking a shorter course, or signing on for 5 more years and completing the course; 5 more years was too much to contemplate and so I settled for a driving course lasting 6 weeks. I thought that this might prove useful and interesting, and would give me a driving licence when I eventually got out, and also the driving school was at Weeton nr. Blackpool, handy for weekends at home.

Home on leave then to await a posting, which I expected to be to Weeton, but nothing so simple, I was on my way down to Northolt in London, and couldn't work out why, nor, as soon became apparent could anyone at Northolt. I booked in, no one knew why I was there but I was soon installed in very comfortable quarters, a detached house with 4 bedrooms I shared with 3 other senior N.C.O.'s, all facilities in the way of hot water available and only a couple of hundred yards away from the mess. Living arrangements completed I quickly visited the accounts dept to make sure I was on the pay roll (this top priority!), and nothing to do then but to await the arrival of instructions as to my next destination. I soon established a routine, and spent my time between my quarters, the mess, and the "Royal George" in Uxbridge, it all seemed very familiar, but after 2 or 3 weeks I was on my way again, this time to Lyneham in Wiltshire, which then was, and still is, a large transport airfield, and I actually thought I was about to resume flying duties, but I was sadly mistaken.

Arrived at Lyneham to find that I was unexpected (again!) and by now I was beginning to think that no one wanted to know me any more, not that I was too concerned, and quickly found myself some comfortable quarters, booked in to the accounts dept. Just to make sure the money kept coming in), and checked out the local geography, i.e. the way to the nearest pub. I then sat back and waited for next development, nice relaxing time really, but I was soon on the move again, and February 1946 found me on my way at last to my driving course.

This proved to be quite enjoyable with a gradual progression from 16hp cars up to 5 ton heavy goods vehicles, the driving part was only 2 hours per day, and I made use of my rank again and did not participate in any of the other activities. I also took advantage of the fact that I was close to home and went there every Friday night for the weekend, all very sociable. Finally passed out, now with a licence to drive anything apart from articulated vehicles, and on my way on leave again to wait to see what my next move would be. I knew at this stage that it wouldn't be long before I was saying goodbye to the RAF, as it was possible to roughly estimate when my number for demobilisation would come up, I thought about mid-summer which turned out to be about right, my number was 41.

The telegram with instructions duly arrived, and I found that I was to report to the M.T. section at 61 M.U. Handforth, this sounded very ideal and I cycled down to book in and make arrangements to live out, thinking this would be a good introduction to civilian life, living at home and cycling to work, but events were to take another, and final turn. However, I introduced myself to the M.T. officer in charge, a gentleman by the name of Quant who took an immediate dislike to me, which was reciprocated, I don't think he really wanted me in his department, difficult for him I suppose as I was still carrying my Warrant Officer rank but now only employed as a driver, but there was nothing he could do about it, my rank was sacrosanct and I was still getting rank pay and flying pay.

I collected the lorry allocated to me, it was a somewhat worse for wear "Canadian 3 ton Dodge" difficult to drive and requiring constant double declutching and gear changing just to get up the smallest of inclines. That said it had to do. and on checking the work schedules I found that there was the odd load to be picked up and taken over to 7 site, which I discovered was in Adlington, where the Industrial Estate is now, which I thought would be ideal for me and so I used my rank again to establish myself as the regular driver covering 7 site. Handforth was overloaded with equipment for storage and made use of several sites over a wide area to store surplus materials, 99%

of which was never used and would end its life in some scrap yard somewhere but it had to be stored and documented. I remember on one occasion taking a load of Lancaster spares to Woodford (Avro's as it was then), at first they refused to accept it but eventually realised they had no alternative, and took it to some far off hangar, they too were getting desperate for space, for no longer required parts were still coming off the production lines.

I made the most of my daily runs to 7 site, usually going home first after collecting my vehicle from the yard and having an early morning break before going to the site to check if there was anything to move before going back to the main site for lunch, another run to Adlington in the afternoon, before returning to the yard, parking up and going home. I often saw the MT officer watching me through his office window and looking quite concerned, don't know why, as although I was usually the last one to leave the yard at the start of the day, I made up for this by being the first one back in the evening. One afternoon a week was given over to vehicle washing, but as there were a few Italian prisoners of war working in the yard, it was quite possible to get a good job done for the price of a packet of cigarettes, with half to get the job started and the other half on completion, it was just a case of sit in the mess until they came to tell me that the job was finished. This rather comfortable period came to a sudden end when I was summoned to see the MT officer to be informed of my next move. He informed me that I was to be posted to Wickenby, which was a storage site for the main depot, to go there and take charge of the MT section. (I think he was pleased to have the opportunity to get rid of me!) My old Dodge had finally given up the previous afternoon, pronounced irreparable and presumably written off, but I was pleased with the replacement, a 2 ton Austin Tender straight from the factory, similar to a pick up and a delight to drive.

I picked the truck up the following morning, called at home to collect my gear, and off to Wickenby, which I ascertained was a disused airfield about 7 miles east of Lincoln. When I arrived it was to discover all signs of flying had long gone, and hangers were full to bursting point with spares that were no longer in demand. On further investigation I discovered that the MT section consisted of one other truck and one driver, a young lad only recently called up. Further enquiries produced some unexpected results, we were a mixed group of about 23 or 24, with 3 cooks, 3 telephonists, and a larger number of armourers making safe and disposing of bombs, ammunition, and other military hardware that was still lying around. I was informed that an administrative officer had been in overall charge until the previous day when he had left to be demobbed, but his replacement had failed to arrive. As a warrant officer with no other senior officers on the station, I had become, De-facto, the commanding officer of the whole establishment, a most unusual situation, but one which was to become quite interesting.

It soon became clear that I was also responsible for seeing that everyone got paid; relieving the telephonist when one of their number was absent on leave, and so providing short term cover, as, although there was very little traffic, the telephone line had to be kept open 24 hours a day, I did make full use of this facility to make a few private calls. Rations were collected every other day from a depot in Market Rasen, and as we were such a small group these were more than adequate, we all dined together and really lived very well. I went over myself for the rations or occasionally sent my one and only driver, there was also daily run to Wragby to pick up any post as postal services were no longer available, Pay day became my responsibility, and involved a trip over to Scampton to collect the money along with a list with the amounts due to everyone, this only happened a couple of times as I was only there a few weeks. On returning with the cash I was wondering how I could get in touch with all as they were scattered around the airfield, I needn't have worried, the bush telegraph had been at work and all and sundry were waiting around the MT office when I returned.

One unusual occurrence that I have a vivid memory of was concerning the main runway, now out of use of course, but there were a team of contractors working at one end making repairs to the surface, whilst at the far end of the same runway were another group engaged in digging it up, taking all the surface material away and ploughing up the land prior to it being returned to agricultural use; this all seemed very odd to say the least, so I enquired as to why the repair work was still going on and I quote "The contract still has 2 years to run", unbelievable! I often wondered what the outcome would be when the 2 groups met, but I was long gone before then.

I made full use of my new found power as MT officer, e.g. I made a habit of driving home for most weekends on Friday evening, arming myself with suitable cover notes to cover my journeys, one for the trip home and another for the return journey on Sunday night, to say that I was picking stores up to take to store at Wickenby. I should perhaps mention that the cover note was a form to cover all transportation, with 3 sections, one requesting transport and saying why needed, this I duly signed as Commanding Officer, the second part to be signed by the MT officer and stamped with the official stamp, this I complied with, and the third part to be signed by the driver on completion of the journey, this I duly signed on my return, and then I filed the form, don't know why!! Fuel was never a problem as I had sole access to the one remaining pump. When I was home for the weekend I parked the lorry in a disused sandpit behind my home in case anyone passing became curious, and on my return on Sunday evening, I stopped off in Lincoln, parked in the station yard, and went into the nearest pub to await the arrival of the last London train, as there were always one or two people travelling up from points south who had been on weekend leave, looking for a lift back to Wickeriby. Generally speaking the whole establishment ran very smoothly, everyone getting on with their own jobs and waiting for the next pay day!

My time at Wickenby passed very quickly and the time when I would part company with the RAF was fast approaching, my demob number (it was 4 1) came up in early June 1946, and the 11th found me on my on my way down to Uxbridge to go through the demobilisation process. I collected my civilian suit (not much choice, there were a lot of look-a-likes walking around), could have a cap or trilby, mac or overcoat, grey or fawn for suit, all parcelled up in a cardboard box. All back pay was collected, plus civilian documents and ration book, uniform handed in apart from that being worn, a one-way ticket for the journey home. Now I was on my way on a month's demob leave, finally severing all links with the RAF in mid July, just before my 24th. Birthday. A final twist when I was on the train on the way to Manchester, an airman got into my compartment, it was my soon to be Brother-in-law, also carrying his little box.

Life in "Civvy Street' was now very close, and I had to seriously rethink my lifestyle, with an immediate 50% reduction in pay, my own clothes and food to buy, and very soon a young family to be responsible for.

On reflection I have to think that my uniform years had been a rewarding experience, having seen and done many things that would have been outside my orbit, but of course I had been very, very lucky, so many of my acquaintances and indeed friends had perished over the skies of Europe. Now it was farewell to the uniform times, and I could finally shape my own destiny about where and when, in short I was no longer just a number.

A. Dudley 2000

F/Lt G.F. Parkinson

A VERY LONG WAY TO CARK

"I was serving in the army in 1942 when I obtained a transfer to the RAF for aircrew training. I had a long rail journey, as I was there in command of a small truck detachment in Elgin, Morayshire. So, my first connection was to Inverness and then an overnight train to London. Here the RAF recruits were housed in 'luxury flats' on the edge of Regents Park. The flats of course had never been used, so we used straw filled palliasses for beds. The sleeping quarters were sited here because the Park grounds and buildings were utilised for parade and kitting out.

I exchanged my khaki for RAF blue and very comfortable poplin shirts. There was some basic 'square bashing', but I was excused as I had passed out from a drill sergeant's course in the army! The weather in August was very hot and humid. I was very pleased to 'skip' pounding the pavements.

We were soon moved to Torbay, where all the large hotels were housing RAF. This posting embraced our Initial Training. I shared a room with another pupil. We all had white "flashes" in the front of our forage caps. An apocryphal joke is as follows:

A Warrant Officer spotted an aircrew pupil with his white flash; "Come here son, what are you?"

"A pupil pilot, Sir,"

"I don't care if you are Pontius Pilot, get yer b****y haircut!"

The course was relatively easy to absorb, and the 'square-bashing' took place on Paignton promenade. The drill sergeant let me take over on some occasions and warned me to "go easy", this is not the army!

Two unexpected sessions were most interesting. One was clay pigeon shooting to illustrate very forcefully how the shooter had to 'lead' the aim in front of the disc - the same skill required in turret firing from an aircraft. The other surprise was a few trips from Torquay harbour to Brixton in pre-war 'pleasure' motor launches. Three or four pupils, plus the local skipper on board used a navigation sea chart inside the cabin. We took compass bearings on shore landmarks and established a moderately accurate plot of our voyage. With some degree of exactness we gave heading instructions to the skipper. We soon realised the fairly calm sea had hidden currents. (In the air, the problem is knowing the wind speed and direction).

I became pally with the drill Sgt who gave me some valuable tips. He suggested it was useful to be one of the top three course pupils as this would have a bearing on the selected country. He was of the opinion that the best choice was S.Africa as there were no freezing winters and more variety of topography. He also moved me in a room to share with 'Paddy'. I soon realised the reason. Paddy was an 'elderly' recruit, about thirty five years and a highly educated Dubliner - an ex college rugby star, a qualified lawyer and a 'five star' raconteur. He was excused all drill and sea trips (he was prone to seasickness). He was the star of the mess where many evenings he would be a super 'stand-up' comic and finish the evening with lead and chorus singing obscene 'rugby songs!' The latter were quite new to my relatively puritan upbringing!

The end of the course came near to the end of Christmas. We had a week's leave and had to report to Blackpool prior to embarkation. I opted for S Africa, which was granted. Blackpool's famous Winter Gardens and ballroom was cleverly utilised to issue tropical clothing. The Quartermaster Sergeant in charge bellowed the hackneyed advice, "If anything fits, bring it back and we'll change it!" I was surprised to have in the wardrobe, a large almost Victorian style pith sun helmet. The same Q/Sgt noting my astonishment said, "When you set sail, chuck the b****r overboard!"

For the few days in Blackpool, we were housed and fed in third rate Boarding Houses. This was a new experience for me, as coming from a fairly wealthy family I had only knowledge of hotel accommodation! From this unwelcome 'brief encounter', we had a short train journey to Liverpool dock where we boarded a troopship; an old ship, about 15,000 tons, oil fired boilers, and a large mess deck, where at 22:00 hours we slung our hammocks for a sleep.

The chilly, damp, January weather made the vision of the Liver building and Custom House look very miserable. Due to the problems of mass handling the convoy north of Belfast, we were anchored mid-Mersey for a full week. At least the anchor chain rattled up its rusty path and with a long siren hoot we eased out of this murky old port.

All at sea

Two days later, the shape and composition of the convoy was clear, all steaming south in the choppy winter waters of the Atlantic, under glowering rain filled clouds. One troop ship in the central area, with small cargo ships on the port and starboard. Two destroyers hunting, always near the perimeter of the formation. Over twenty ships in all. The pack changing course every hour or so to fox the German subs. Unfortunately, we were limited in progress, as the slowest freighter set the pace.

Our ship's compliment was about one hundred RAF and four hundred army types en route to help the N.African War. The mess deck had long trestle tables where we were served with lukewarm basic food.

My mess table 'crew' was making heavy weather, trying to make a neat exercise when getting in or out of their hammocks. When I was fourteen I sailed on a school sponsored cruised in the Baltic. The ship was almost identical to our troopship, so I had fifteen days to perfect a stylish gymnastic movement to master the hammock problem!

After passing the Canaries, the weather improved with spells of warm sunshine. We were settling into a routine and coping with saltwater shaving and monotonous seascapes – and the food. When we gradually tacked to port with an easterly heading, it was obvious that Freetown would be a change of scenery.

We dropped anchor in Freetown bay. Dead calm, with heavy cloud. The air was stifling, seemed like 100% humidity. Many decided to try and sleep on the deck. The second day was a huge success! A black cloud shrouded the area and around 16:00 hours an almighty tropical thunderstorm crashed into action. Raindrops like we had never seen, and almost to a man we stripped off and lathered our bodies from head to toe. The decks became a mass of white foam!

The following morning the anchor chain rattled its clarion call and a cheer went up from the motley collection of well cleaned troops! Heading south once more, we knew we had passed the half way mark (for the RAF but not the army). Four weeks from leaving the Mersey, we noticed our 'Chef' was delivering a potage of rice in every meal. We soon came to one conclusion: we had run out of palatable food! A few days later we fully understood the slang word 'grub' - most of the rice was riddled with maggots! The situation was grim as we had very little safe food for the next two weeks. Most of us were almost shrinking daily.

The safari begins

At last! Gently moving into Cape Town harbour was an amazing sight; brilliant sunshine lighting every crag and crevice of the near vertical face of Table Mountain. This three thousand foot mountain dominates the city making the city hall and prominent buildings look like scale models.

The RAF was allowed off first and a mad rush headed for the Red Cross Service building near the docks. Bacon, eggs, fried bread was at that moment true Ambrosia! After filling our starved innards, I was approached by a lady who offered to take four of us on a tour of the Cape Peninsula. The rest of the day was a superb guided trip of over thirty miles. On day two, a few of us caught the electric train to the Indian Ocean side of the city. Here was excellent bathing in water over 70 degrees.

On day three at 15:30 hours we boarded the train. This was for all of us the longest train journey – 11,00 miles to Pretoria. The coaches were very good for a 3 feet 6 inches gauge (essential to cope with severe curves). Each compartment had two 'pull-out' beds. Our kit bags made a problem. We were glad to have thrown the stupid pith helmets in the Atlantic!

We soon steamed through Paarl and on into the Cape vineyard country. The small town of Woicester was the last 'outpost' of the cultivated areas, lying in the shadow of the massive sandstone Hex River mountains at over 6,000 feet. The two 'Pacific' type locos began their hard serpentine climb through the Hex River valley. Rock towers on each side of the track. Before nightfall we gained over 3,000 feet on to the Great Kariou, or High Veldt. The scenery was a seismic change from the lush Western Cape. The grass was a parched yellow with off rocky outcrops. This plain stretches hundreds of miles with a few very small towns and villages. Sheep farming and maize was the primary agrarian activity.

In the night we probably stopped for water and crew replacement. In the morning we realised we had passed Kimberly the giant diamond mine before dawn. We had a good breakfast with an exotic porridge! This was dark brown made from unrefined maize ('mealie') very tasty, quite different from oats. We crawled past the ghostly shanty town of Soweto on the western edge of Johannesburg. Then the strange sights of huge pyramid piles of grey waste dug from the deep gold mines drilled into the Witwatersrand granite.

We travelled non-stop through the city – another twenty miles to Pretoria. After twenty two hours we walked on 'dry land'! A few trucks carted us uphill to a bleak S.African Army barracks. This was our home for a few weeks. From here the various aircrew types, pilots, navigators, gunners and so on, would be posted to different airfields, mostly in the Transvaal State.

Afrikaanerland

In our first week we had three lectures by a RAF Officer. This was an intensive history lesson of the country and pitfalls to avoid. Although most of the wealth and infrastructure had been developed by British investors and know-how, most of the agricultural land was occupied by Afrikaner, or Boer farmers. The large retail stores and cinemas were very much a Jewish preserve. In the 1940's Johannesburg had a derogatory and racist name of 'Jewburg' (the Jewish population being over 10%). The Afrikaner population was 67%

of the Whites and dominated the government. The Blacks outnumbered the Whites and 'Coloureds' by at least 3:1.

Many Afrikaners hated the British. We had erected 'concentration' camps in the Boer War, where many women and children died. Our army burnt many Boer farms. We were warned not to hitch hike, as several RAF had been abducted or run-over! Any golfers should ignore any road signs, "HOU LINKS", because this means "Keep Left"!

We were assured that all food and water was safe to drink. We also had RAF medical staff available for any serious injury or illness. Malaria had been 'tamed' and snake bites were very rare. Some of our instructors would be members of the S.African army, and were 'pro-British'!

Food

Most of our meals were similar to British fare with a few exceptions, the only potato was sweet potato. Steaks were abundant. Our bread could be rye flour or mixed. Apparently 'Lion' beer was like US 'Budweiser' and brandy was dirt cheap.

Laundry

On the airfields we would have native ('Black') families who collected each bundle and would be paid 5d plus a bar of soap!

Pretoria & Jo'burg

Pretoria is the government capital. The centre could be truly described as pretty. A fine central avenue lined with superb jacaranda trees with a profusion of lilac blossom. At one end, well elevated, is an imposing government building using pleasing red sandstone. Johannesburg is quite the opposite. It looks like a small American city; concrete apartments and office blocks, eight or ten floors. A fine park with zoo breaks up the unimposing built-up areas.

In 1940 these cities could be regarded as relatively 'new', as S Africa only became a true republican country thirty years earlier after the 1910 Act of Union. In 1939 Jan Smuts became the Prime Minister. He was a great statesman who gave Churchill his full support, especially in his 'darkest hours'. Without Smuts, there would not have been any RAF aircrew training inside S Africa.

Training in an exotic location
with climbing opportunities
an added bonus!

Cathedral Peak Hotel, Winterton.

1. Approaching summit of Cathedral Peak 9200ft. Red sandstone top crags..

2. Looking into Drakenberg panorama. Highest Champagne Castle 11400ft. Visibility about 70 miles.

3. Fine view of Cathedral Peak, The bell and two horns. Most of ridge about 10,000ft

4. Zulu family. Males probably in gold mines on 12 mth contract.

5. Our hotel in Cathedral Peak Valley.

6. A day in the saddle, Basuto ponies very nimble and took us up 500ft pass into Basutoland.

7. Head of Cathedral Peak Valley. Ponies drinking crystal clear water

8. Bottom of a 400ft granite Kloot. Transvaal

9. Top 100ft same Kloot

10. Perfect rough granite. Top of a large outcrop about 200ft

11. Our small hotel, 35 miles from Durban. 200 yards to beach about four hotels in 1940s

12. Indian Ocean. Sea temps 75f. Note large cars parked.

13. Late afternoon rain, Perfect sand. Surf about 3-4ft

14. Our first week in S.Africa. Afternoon winter sunshine in the Pretoria holding barracks

Elementary flying school

This was on a converted meadow on the edge of a very small mining town about twelve miles east of Johannesburg city centre. We were twenty four strong and 'rarin' to go'. The aircraft were two-seater Tiger Moths, an old trusted and tested biplane. My instructor was an English speaking S African Army flyer. His first piece of information was the fact that the field was rather bumpy and our altitude was over 5,000 feet. This required the engine to work hard for take-off and climbing. He also pointed out that landing in the thin air gave rise to floating instead of a nice comfortable 'three point' landing with wheel and tail settling down 'sans crunch'

We all found the controls very sensitive and forward view restricted. The first few hours were mostly taken up with 'circuits and bumps' and how to make accurate turns. This course was twelve weeks duration. In week three, after two take-offs and landings, my instructor taxied to the perimeter, climbing out he tapped on my helmet and shouted, "It's all yours, don't bend the b----r, on your way!" So after carefully setting the controls for take-off, I started my FIRST SOLO! Full throttle and climbing to 500 feet, turn left, then fly parallel to the field; line up and nose down for a good approach at around 85m.p.h. Ease back on the stick, lean out of cockpit and cut throttle – a fair

DH Tiger Moth

non bumpy landing! Taxi back, soaked in sweat and ready for lunch with a steak!

Our entire course soloed after 7½ to 9 hours. Two weeks later, one of our clan tried a steep turn when solo and spun in to his death; a very sobering day. All flying was stopped for twenty four hours in respect.

The weeks rolled by which included the full repertoire of flying problems: tight turns, spins, aerobatics, cross-country routes and night flying plus ground instruction.

The climate

As winter approached we were informed that on the High Veldt this was the dry season with hardly any rain. We could expect two or three weeks of cloudy days, when a moist air mass was pushed up the Limpopo valley from the Indian Ocean. Most days were bright warm sunshine with chilly nights; excellent visibility and ideal for flying. The summer weather would be much hotter in the afternoons. Occasionally there would be thunderstorms and heavy rain, usually in the mid to late afternoon.

The mountain club

One day my instructor - when we were having our 'elevenses' of a wedge of rye bread toast and a huge mug of black coffee - asked me if I would like to join the Transvaal section of the S African Mountain Club. He had heard of my pre-war exploits on the British crags. I leapt at this hint and the week-end saw me meeting Tony Hooper in Jo'burg. He was the local secretary and he was delighted to have one on board, as several male members were now in the S African Army. He was a bachelor and lived in a small flat in central Jo'burg and was employed by a gold mine as a Cost Accountant. He was a Kiwi and he emigrated around 1930 to Derby to work at Rolls Royce. He moved to S Africa in 1935. We set off on the Sunday in his six-cylinder Dodge car to a granite ridge forty miles north of Pretoria. Here we met about a dozen members with four very fit young women. Two were PT instructors in 'posh' girls' schools. The crags were about 150-200 feet and provided several routes. After a few hours climbing Tony made me a leader!

I soon found that this coterie was a veritable 'Foreign Legion'. There were three German Jews. Emil from Berlin was a skilled gold engraver and emigrated to S Africa in the early 1930's. The other two, Hans and his wife Elsa, were expert climbers from Munich with the Bavarian Alps on their 'doorstep'. They had escaped the Nazis in 1936. A forty year old Texan, (a mining drill engineer), had climbed in the Sierra. To complete this pot-pourri, we had 6ft 2ins 'Tiny' who had a Swiss mother and Afrikaner father. He could speak English, Afrikaans, Dutch and German.

Emil the gold engraver became a very good friend. Due to his years of experience in the gold jewellery trade he encouraged me to invest as much spare cash I could raise. Over a period of some months, he showed me what he considered were bargains. He produced somehow, a superb collection of 18 carat solid gold Swiss watches and various sizes of 22 carat wedding rings.

He was confident that I would find willing buyers back in England and a handsome profit. He gave me valuable tips on selling tactics – in no way offer them to retailers! I followed his tactics and on returning to my home town of Bolton, I found a very wealthy cotton mill owner who 'doubled' my money. He would give the watches to his best customers for Christmas and rings to his girl employees, as wedding bells were in the offing!

Hans and Elsa lived in the same block as Tony. To my great pleasure they suggested I stay with them on alternate weekends, with Tony filling in the balance. The best 'Safari' was an extended week-end New Year where we could camp out three nights. Tony arranged, by some magic, to contact a retired Indian Army Colonel who owned over 1,000 acres with a superb farm and massive ranks of citrus trees. Behind his farm was a steep hillside which was the rim of a large Kloof (Canyon). This was perfect rock descending nearly 500 feet to a river below. The Colonel brought with him three 'bearers', cases of peach brandy, 'Lion' beer and a case of white wine! Each night we lit a camp fire and the second night we shared with two inquisitive baboons!

Four or five climbers thought their idyllic life would come to an end when violence against the White population began and increased in the late 1950's. Six did emigrate to England around 1960. I bumped into Tony one evening wearing a bowler hat on Euston Station's Concourse! Hans volunteered for air gunnery and flew over Italy with the S African Air force and fortunately survived.

Advance flying school

We moved four miles further east to Nigel, another small mining community. The field was mostly bare red earth and was a large area but not level. Our number had dwindled to eighteen due to some being diverted to another station where they flew single engine planes. Our posting was to fly twin-engine Airspeed Oxfords. The change from the delicate Tiger Moths was a great shock – like moving from a Fiesta to a three ton truck.

Before starting this six month course we were granted a seven day leave. I was part of a foursome where the other three were also Lancastrians and keen fell walkers. We opted for a 'frontal attack' on the main peaks of the Natal Drakensberg. We stayed in the Cathedral Peak Hotel; a small stone building with basic wood chalets (4 beds each). The valley was awesome, over six peaks looming up, ranging from 9,500 to 11,000 feet. The tops were spectacular rosy red sandstone with snow in the gullies. We had perfect weather and climbed four peaks. The adjacent valley was the site where the great 'Zulu' film was produced.

Airspeed Oxford

Flying the Oxfords we soon realised we were in rarefied air. The take-off was a long, bumpy, roaring mass of striving machinery before we dare ease back the control wheel. Landing was even worse, especially after noon. The hot earth develops severe convection draughts. Gradually we learned to man handle these bucking beasts and tamed them in the air.

Except for aerobatics, the regime was very similar to the Tiger Moth syllabus, but additional skills were demanded for bombing, formation flying, long cross-country and plenty of night flying. I had persuaded the Lancashire lads of the possibility that if we obtained high marks, we could select our preferences. During the last week, we were all interviewed by the C/O. Our preferred posting was for flying boats in Coastal Command. To our amazement this was granted.

Durban and surf

When we were staying in the Cathedral Peak Hotel, we met a charming lady who owned a small hotel on the coast near Durban. She urged us to visit her on our next leave. Hence we headed south on the electric line to Durban for our seven day post Advance Flying School month's leave.

We were required to take a short train out of Durban to a small resort. The railway line traversed westwards, with the sea on one side and sugar plantations on the other. The climate here is almost identical to Florida, a sub-tropical hot humid climate with regular rain fall, often from thunder storms.

The sugar saga was very amusing. The British pioneers dreamed of another Jamaica, so plantations were generated and mills built for processing. One snag: the natives usually sent their wives (plural) to work and cutting cane was beyond their feminine muscles. The British, unlike the Afrikaners were never short of money-making ideas! To this end Indians were shipped in from Bombay and Calcutta! The sugar industry thrived and so did the Indians. The supreme irony was the 'Cinema'. One Indian family pooled their resources and by 1940 were quite rich. So much so, they owned the best cinema in Durban, but due to Afrikaner race laws, they were NOT legally allowed to sit in it!

The holiday was a huge success. The hotel was surrounded by palm trees and tropical flowering bushes. Two tennis courts were almost on the beach. There was a short stretch of 'sea washed' turf, then some gold sand and then three to four feet of surf. Not at all like Blackpool or Morecambe! Even more strange to us was our night time 'skinny-dips'. The night temperatures were around 70F. When our evening meal had 'settled', we headed for the beach. The sea temperature was nudging 80F; a legacy from the Indian Ocean current sweeping down between Madagascar and the mainland.

Racism

Before I left the Pretoria barracks, I suffered a strange and very painful experience. In the two or three days prior to my embarkation leave we had a rudimentary medical check; this included a visit to the dental clinic. I was given a temporary filling in a canine tooth. The dentist told me to have this tooth repaired in S Africa.

In the second week in the barracks I reported to the sick bay where an Afrikaner Army dentist completed the filling. During the night I had vague aches round my head and by dawn I was feverish. Two of my friends collected a wheelchair from the Sick Bay. I was transferred to a bed and was checked over and soon fed a succession of drugs. The following day my temperature was hovering over 104F. The senior nurse felt my mouth area and the canine was painful. She returned around noon and explained she had arranged for a RAF dentist to come to the clinic. She added that he was a Harley Street consultant on a S African monitoring tour.

In due course, he examined my tooth and immediately commenced operating and carefully removed the new filling. After what seemed like hours he exclaimed, "You've been poisoned!" He then gave a semi-technical dissertation regarding the apparent normal filling. He was raging mad and for all to hear claimed he would send a report to the S African Army H.Q.

and to the S African Dentists' Association. I gathered the Afrikaner had packed in some toxic compound and 'trapped' this with an innocent looking amalgam! This incident was a vivid wake-up call stressing the unpleasant fact that not all the RAF's enemies were Nazis.

The above was a rare extreme inbuilt hatred of the British. Bear in mind the S African Army produced two divisions serving in N Africa in the 8th Army. One was decimated at Tobruk. Most of the senior Officers were Afrikaners. In our aircrew RAF Stations, there was always a minority of S Africans.

The essential racist problem was the Whites versus Blacks. Most of Africa was colonised, where universally the White Europeans considered themselves as superior to the Blacks. A term of almost endearment was "Boy!" Many British colonies were well run and few cases of extreme cruelty occurred. Rhodesia north of S Africa had many large farms (maize, tobacco, ranching) where several Negro families had modest accommodation with some basic education for the children. In S Africa, however, most farms were owned by Afrikaners and relatively small. Very often the farm labourers were poorly housed and often maltreated. In the 1940's typical punishment for the owner was a fine of £5 for injuring a Black and £10 if the unfortunate servant died.

Many small High Veed villages had a Dutch Reform church. No Blacks allowed inside (similar to many US churches). A typical Sunday morning would see farmers with wife and children, dressed in black riding to church on a horse drawn 'buggy'.

S Africa is 'multi-coloured'. In Natal many Indians had developed small retail shops selling to Blacks and they often provided labour in hotels or on the railways. A large number of 'Coloureds' existed in the West Cape. These were mixed breeds dating back to early maritime contacts with European sailors visiting Cape Town. Hotel labour was also common. Only 'pure' White's had a vote or respectable work and housing. Most Europeans living in the suburbs had one to three servants, usually living in a concrete 'house' at the end of the garden. The White children nearly always had a Black nursemaid. The White wives had a very easy life with no chores or child care activities.

Large numbers of Blacks lived in segregated shanty-towns called townships. They had to have an official pass if they worked in the White city areas or attempted to move to another town.

The most obvious rampant racism was the viciousness of the police. This was especially visible in Johannesburg. In the early days of the War, the civic authorities found to their horror that many policemen were members of an extreme Fascist organisation! These fanatics had their own Nazi type uniforms and badges. They met at weekends in secluded parts of the Veld. This mob was fired and hurriedly fresh recruits were drafted in. This 'dilution' may have lowered the average quality of the force.

Typical actions clear to see were pushing Blacks off pavements, arresting any Black with no pass and much worse was the frequency of Blacks 'run over' by police cars on patrol. The poor quality of police was still visible in the years of apartheid.

Some of the legacy of the above racism has seen the huge number of poor Afrikaner farmers in N Transraal murdered by local Blacks, often labourers of the farmer. A subtle by-product of endemic racism was how the White society hid or absorbed poor Whites. There was no 'dole' or benefits system, so the small number of poorly educated or mentally impaired (Afrikaners) usually had jobs available on the State Railway: porter, guards, shunting etc. Extreme cases usually alcoholics, would beg in the city centre, often carted off to nearest police station. I have no information how they 'hide' poverty in today's 'Rainbow State' - A very complex and uneasy society.

Reconnaissance navigation school

All Coastal Command pilots had to pass the special course of over-sea navigation and allied subjects. This was based on a field on the south coast edge outside a village named George (today it is a modern town with an industrial section and a motorway leading 300 miles to Cape Town!). Behind George is a 4,000 foot mountain which we soon climbed. The course was twelve weeks and quite intensive. The Lancashire lads combined resources and here we flew in pairs, taking turns at the chart table fitted in the Avro Ansons. All the instructors were RAF and very good.

Two highlights occurred. One was when we spotted the 'Queen Mary' in grey paint heading for Durban and then en route to Egypt. The second was a weekend in Oudtshoorm. This is a strange place trapped in a narrow valley between our local mountains and the edge of the Karoo. Almost desert climate, very hot and cactus like Arizona. Ostrich farms provided feathers. There is a huge cave. The train journey has lots of curves to climb above sea level and 10-15 mph is about as much as the old steam locos could manage.

We passed out with 'flying colours' and were sent to a holding camp at the foot of Table Mountain. Albeit the same latitude, we were now in the West Cape winter. This is mild weather with frequent drizzle or light rain. The 'Tablecloth' of low cloud often shrouded the summit. The climate on the George area of the coast is regarded as the most benign on the world.

For twelve months there is no definite summer or winter. Rain is light and infrequent; usually sufficient to maintain a lush green environment. Much of this coast is dubbed 'The Garden Route' and is a popular resort area for tourists. However, the damp weather restricted my climbing activities and I only squeezed in one good climb with two University rock climbers.

No convoy

The Lancashire lads were informed that when a suitable ship arrived, we would be moved to Bahama to convert on to Catalinas, US built long range flying boats.

In due course we had a lift in a truck to the docks where we boarded the "Athlone Castle". This was a fine ship of about 25,000 tons and one of the fleet of Union Castle Liners. They sailed pre-war from England, round the Cape to India, and north up Africa's east coast. They carried mail – two weeks (or so we were told) UK to Cape Town. In the late afternoon we eased out of Cape Town and before nightfall we had a wonderful sight of the setting sun outlining the twenty miles of the peninsula; a truly magnificent sea and landscape.

The passengers on board gave us a shock. Just a handful of American Army personnel 'rattled' around the lower decks. They had all suffered physical or mental injuries. Our quarters were on the top deck in a large cabin with eight bunks. The ship had left Bombay, so we assumed the Americans had been bombed by the Japs, or had contracted fevers. We had no idea where we would land. After three weeks of fast sailing (occasional zigzags) we slowly steamed one morning into New York harbour! We could see the famous building 'in the flesh'. Woolworth, Chrysler and high rise apartment or office blocks in profusion.

The Americans were offloaded, but we had to wait hours, because the 'paperwork' was not working smoothly. Eventually we boarded a small launch which cruised out of the docks and sailed about ten miles to a small island between the mainland and Long Island. This was a well-built barracks used by the US Army to train young cadets who would be commissioned. Our sleeping quarters were within a dormitory. We were amazed with the weather; hellish hot and humid all day and night. Also mosquitos during the night! This was the end of August. We were told that heat waves could last weeks and everyone was eagerly waiting for a thunderstorm!

Our first day in the US of A! We decided the best action was to contact the Adjutant. He was mystified and apparently it was good luck he had four spare beds! He wisely directed us to go into the city and harangue the British

Embassy. In the meantime, he handed us a few dollars to enable us to pay our way once in the city. He also gave us rail tickets which would give us free train service to and from our 'camp' main live station.

So in the steaming heat of New York, we arrived in the famous Times Square Railway Station. Two levels of underground platforms and a vast circular concourse. The Embassy was a slow and weary experience. We were for the time being 'lost' in the USA! They were more generous with dollars than our adjutant's offer. We had to report to a specified officer three days hence and not to go beyond 48 hours' notice.

Not knowing when we would move out we decided to see the sights within a few days. We had a letter from the Embassy stating who we were etc. With this epistle we approached a Red Cross information department near Broadway. One attractive and obviously well-educated young woman took pity on us and offered to arrange a week's itinerary! After sampling a ghastly 'eat joint', we reported to our guide. So in quick succession we shot up the Empire State skyscraper and then visited the Rockefeller Centre where there was a vaudeville theatre with chorus girls. Everyone had to be at least 5ft 9ins, as the stage was so large. Then Yankee Stadium's strange baseball game, a boat tour of the bay, Wall Street and a peep inside the Stock Exchange and last of all, a party in her luxurious flat in Lexington Avenue.

We met journalists and a Red Indian photographer for 'Life' magazine. We had to answer a barrage of questions about Britain and our travels in Africa. The 'Life' man gave us an offer to go with him on a day's 'shoot' on Long Island. The venue was to take photos of the super wealthy with their yachts and where possible their mansions. The Native American was a very dynamic and imposing man. He had 'done' the Pacific War with a mass of shots in the thick of island invasions. Hoping to get to England before the allies invaded France; he picked our brains until we were mentally exhausted.

Our friend organised three weekend visits to quite different families. Mr Lovejoy (apt name) was a Texas oil tycoon. His family lived on Long Island; he worked in his Wall Street Office. He was a tough very sociable bod and had worked very hard all his life. His wife and teenage children were nauseous! They had three Black servants, a private boat jetty and a shared private aircraft in Texas. Another family had their wealth in a large clothing factory in the NY 'Garment Centre'. We met them in their weekend second home in the Adirondack Mountains; lovely spot but too many powerful mosquitos. Almost all garment millionaires were Jewish. Our hosts were from Russian parents. Very modest man and very well educated children. They were extremely keen on learning about the UK and the possible outcome of the War. The third family also had a weekend home about fifty miles north of the city in a pleasant beach house. The host was a science Professor in one of the NY Universities. His wife was also an academic and assisted her husband in research. One son, who was very bright, was hoping for Harvard. They were well versed in the War and asked a string of questions regarding our RAF experiences; the very best of America.

At last our American experience came to an end when we were directed to the docks. Here was a huge ex Italian liner gutted for troop carrying. Zillions of US Army troops squeezed in. We were on the top deck which contained US Officers and twenty four attractive Red Cross girls. Our 'entente cordiale' was very!

Within six days we crawled into Liverpool. Just like when we left: grey, wet and dirty. Everything seemed strange after our long safari. I never did fly Catalinas and after further navigational specialisation if found myself at RAF Cark!

Cark airfield

Considering the urgency and strict budget, the Cark airfield was cleverly 'slotted' into the available land area. On the north perimeter is the fishing village of Flookburgh and the railway line. To the east is Humphrey Head, and of course on the south rim is the coastal edge of the Kent estuary. Similar airfields were made in a ring around the Irish Sea. Walney, Millom, Dumfries, Jurby I of M, N Ireland and a few more specialised airfields such as Silloth, Campbeltown, Blackpool and Valley in Anglesey.

These sites were very valuable due to their position on the north-west coasts of England. Further away form 'easy' targets in the south. In addition, training routes could easily be planned over the sea to avoid high ground and flying over large towns. Most of these airfields were used by Training Command. The trainees would in most cases be posted to Bomber Command as Pilots, Navigators, Bomb Aimers, Wireless Operators and Gunners.

The Cark runways were level, with No 1 set for heading into the prevailing SW winds. The No 2 runway was not often used due to its N-S direction. All the runways were fitted with the standard night lighting which was a clever design.

On the western edge of the field was a dead straight lane leading from Flookburgh village square right into the beach; essential for the horse drawn carts going out into the sea for shrimps, or flat fish. This lane became an integral part of the field, giving personnel easy access to the aircraft, lecture rooms and hangers. Most of the living quarters and communal buildings were in the N W sector close to Flookburgh. The WAAF quarters were rather isolated! Some of the amenities included a gym, cinema and squash courts. The main line, Barrow to Carnforth, was a fifteen minute hike, or a few minutes by bike. Unusually, the War Department planners had squeezed into the south west corner between the fishermen's lane and perimeter track, a small army artillery detachment camp.

By luck and certainly not by design, the small town of Grange-over-Sands was within a fifteen minute bike ride. For a period during the War, The Grand Hotel 100 rooms) was home to training courses for RAF clerical duties. The Grange Village Hall and the Grand Hotel ballroom held regular dances. Another lucky twist of topography is the proximity of Kendal - about twelve miles. Bus services were available and the town's amenities included good pubs, cinema and library. For the more adventurous, further afield were Lancaster and Morecambe.

The popularity rating of the station will never be known; the pupils had a different viewpoint from the permanent Staff. They were 'passing birds' and most of these airmen had only a fleeting interest in the nearby countryside or towns. The few in the Staff who were southerners usually regarded Cark as a "God forsaken dump soaked in rain!"

Cark's 'job description'

In the second half of the War, RAF Cark developed a very good intensive six week navigation course. The trainees were newly qualified pilots, who had been trained mostly in Canada, or other Empire countries.

The concept was two-fold. Firstly, the weather and flying conditions in W Europe are very different from the stable weather conditions prevailing in their areas of training. Secondly, most of these pilots would be posted to heavy bombers and would be the crew's captain. The close association between the navigator and pilot was essential. Prior to the Cark courses, pilots had very limited knowledge about navigation problems.

The huge expansion of the 'Empire Training' Scheme assessed a substantial flow of qualified pilots arriving in the UK. Very different from the desperate years of 1939/42 when shortages of trained crews and planes was a grave problem.

The course gave the pilots a rudimentary knowledge of practical dead reckoning navigation, together with basic meteorological/weather problems. In winter months, most courses had a fair share of bad weather. Our Staff pilots and maintenance crews played a big part in the success of the operations. In my 'watch' we had no mechanical or structural failures and to my knowledge, no staff pilot was 'fired'.

The aircraft used was the great Avro Anson with two engines and room for four crew members. A very reliable and safe aircraft used across the Empire and Training Command was well equipped with these faithful 'workhorses'. At least six airfields on the Irish Sea coasts had fleets of these planes for many long years.

Where We Flew

From Cark we had the options of several routes and these were varied during each course. The forecast weather often had to be considered before a route could be selected.

Typical routes were:

Cark – Mull of Galloway – Mts of Mourne – Calf of Man.

Cark – Blackpool Tower – Holyhead – Calf of Man

Cark – Carlisle – Mull of Galloway – Walney – Cark

Each day we flew, the instructors had to confer with the duty Met Officer (we had two full time WAAF Officers). If a flight was leaving am we had limited meteorological readings as only a handful of stations were West of Cark. A rough isobar map was drawn and our 'conference' had to use a lot of guess work. Our score for forecasting time of rain was very good. We also had to use care and cancel flying if the signs were poor. Low cloud and strong gusty winds were usually cause for cancellation.

The planned routes were designed for durations of three to four hours. Safety was the key factor. One advantage of the geographical position of Cark was the short distance from Walney Island. You could always see the white sea and beach edge of the island, even on a dark night. Once the island edge is seen, an easy run up the estuary to Cark was available and bacon and eggs ready for the crews if coming home from a night flight! If the weather turned really nasty we could land at Walney rather than risk hitting Hampsfell near Cark.

Gibb's airforce

The C/O of RAF Cark was a larger than life bod, named W/C Gibb. A peace time RAF Officer, who was on reserve list and living in Jamaica 1939. He was a tall handsome man of about 45 years and developed an amazing style and flair, which gave him almost carte blanche access to running Cark in a unique manner. So much so, some of the 'old lags' of Cark christened the initials GAF to stand for "Gibbs Air Force!"

I was an experienced rock climber. 'Gibby' asked me if I would like to add Mountain Rescue to my duties. This was agreed and within a week we received two near new Jeeps courtesy of Burtonwood US base! You will see from my notes that we never had to perform many rescues, but we had to have trials, so a group of ex climbers had rapid transport to Langdale, Coniston and other craggy meccas! We became better climbers than navigators.

'Gibby' had wangled somehow, a two-seater Miles Magister trainer. On a fine Sunday morning he would often 'beat up' the airfield and try some aerobatics over the bay! He would organise parties in the Officers' Mess and local young ladies could be invited. The Jeeps were useful taxis and one evening we collected several WAAF Officers who were trainees in the Old England Hotel, Bowness.

The best 'wangle' was in mid-Summer, when he authorised an exchange food barter system. The scheme was classic. During one of our training flights, the pilot was instructed to have 'engine trouble' and land at Jurby, Isle of Man. On board would be several large fresh salmon from the River Kent and estuary. We swapped this load for fresh hand- picked strawberries! Of course the C/O of Jurby was happy to oblige.

One week in 1944 we suddenly had about 60 Italian POW dumped on us. The head WAAF Officer at this time was a well-educated, tall fine looking woman about 30 years and disciplined her flock very well and made a lot of effort to keep unwanted pregnancies to a very low figure.

About 48 hours after the Prisoners Of War arrived, our "Queen Bee" (WAAF C/O) came into the Mess about 6 pm white with rage and generally not happy. Apparently 'Gibby' had ordered her to muster all the WAFF's into No 1 Hanger. He gave them a lecture on the sexual appetite of the Italians and how they should avoid these men at all costs. Our enraged 'Queen Bee' was certain that many of her girls would succumb to the Latin lovers!

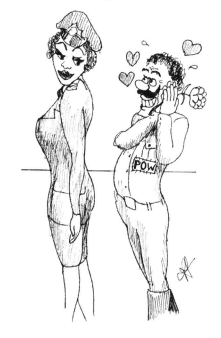

On a more serious plane, when we were notified an airman had been killed and was to be buried in any of the local areas, 'Gibby' promptly laid on a full funeral party. It was appreciated by the next of kin and friends of the deceased.

On one occasion he gave me a very delicate mission. One of the Cark mechanics had developed a relationship with the wife of a wealthy Army Officer serving in the Middle East. When this Officer returned he found the tools for his Aston Martin sports car were missing. I had to smooth out this Officer and gave him regards from 'Gibby', that we would consult the police to retrieve these tools as soon as possible – not a pleasant visit.

When the atom bomb was dropped, we knew that RAF Cark would soon be redundant. 'Gibby' wasted no time in designing several items of furniture to be made by the joiners in the maintenance crews. The wood was pine, used in the construction of massive planks forming huge crates holding spare engines and other parts for the 'Flying Fortress' bombers. His useful contacts within the giant Burtonwood US base provided a great source of free wood! The joiner lads were happy to show their skills in cabinet making – an attractive change from 'messing about' with Ansons.

'Gibby' went too far when he fancied extracting a large section of carpet from the Officers' Mess. We believe the Adjutant claimed there was an inventory of buildings and fittings, this curbed his excesses.

Some historians believe he emigrated to Rhodesia and was killed in an accident. In conclusion, he was a great 'character' and basically a true gentleman with the efficiency of the station and well-being of his hundreds of crew uppermost in his mind.

The ansons – 'workhorses'

The Avro Anson was designed and made by the famous company who made the great Lancaster bombers. This aircraft was an old design and initially in the 1930's was a small bomber. At the outbreak of War the Wellington twin engine bomber was much larger and powerful. The Anson was soon

W/Cdr Gibb & Sqd /Ldr Skingsley with Magister trainer

established as a superb training aircraft. It was reliable, safe, easy to fly, capacious body, room for four or five crew and an air cooled engine, easier to maintain than liquid cooled (as for R R Merlins).

Training Command used the Ansons for training, navigators, wireless operators, bomb-aimers, gunners and of course, all the Ansons used for these functions required safe and accurate pilots. Many were shipped out to Canada and Africa as part of the huge Empire training scheme.

Avro Anson Mk1

The operating speeds were relatively slow, which was a great safety factor. Typical cruising speed was 120 mph; the take-off speed is usually about 90 mph. This speed is reduced for gentle climbs. For landing, a typical speed on the final approach with wheels down is about 70 mph. At touch down the engine is throttled back in an attempt to make a three-point landing.

On twin engine aircraft, a vital part of the performance is the ability to fly level safely on one engine in emergencies. The Anson (if not overloaded) will fly at 90 mph. If an engine fails on take-off, the situation is very different and demands on the pilot increase dramatically. If the undercarriage has not been wound up, the pilot will not be able to climb. When the undercarriage is up, a slow climb may be possible. Fortunately, the Cheetah engines were very reliable.

An aircraft, is it like driving a car?

NO! There is one common factor. Keep alert to keep alive. Some people latch on to the idea of steering. In a car you simply turn the wheel to the left and the car obeys and also turns. In flying, the control 'wheel' or stick is also moved to the left for a left (port) turn. However, we can now compare the extreme. If the car travels too fast into a bend, the result will be a skid, or at worst will turn over, or hit a roadside obstacle. Let us assume the pilot is in his Spitfire flying at 20,000 feet above the English Channel. No trees or walls up here! The period is 1940, and to his horror our pilot hears some 'pings' as bullets from a ME109 ricocheting off his Merlin engine!

In a panic he lunges his stick to the left to avoid further target practice for his German foe. Forgetting all the instruction he has recently received from a seasoned flyer, due to a sudden severe 'G' force, he has a black-out; two seconds later he is recovering sight, when even more horror - the Spitfire is now in a spin heading down at considerable speed. An easier target for the ME109!

Unlike the car, the plane is not on wheels gripping the road due to friction between tyre and road surface. The aircraft has to support itself in air, not on air. The essential structural components are the wing, tail plane and rudder. The engine(s) provide the thrust, the power to propel the aircraft in a forward direction. The section of the wing (shape and size) and the tail plane are designed by highly skilled engineers. The air flowing past the wing and tail generates a 'lift' force keeping the plane airborne. Modern jet fighters have so much power they can execute vertical climbs. In the days of propeller driven planes, no such configuration was possible.

Reverting back to our disastrous tight turn to port, the pilot had not had sufficient experience to develop reflex actions whereby he would move his control smoothly and apply left rudder (left foot) and at the same time increase his power (throttle lever forward). All these three actions conducted at the same time and in harmony. Not quite as simple as turning a car steering wheel a couple of turns!

So far, we have been flying in the horizontal mode, with the airflow nicely balanced between wing and tail plane. By easing the control forward we create a dive and pull back to climb. These movements actuate the ailerons on the tail plane altering the original airflow. Usually when setting a descent, the power is reduced and vice versa for climbing. In highly manoeuvrable aircraft such as Spitfires, the control stick can be moved in a huge variety of positions, for example, forward and to left which is essential for a diving turn. In effect the aircraft is in a three dimensional environment, quite different from a car which is two dimensional as it is always in horizontal mode.

Now we should consider two key elements to our control of the aircraft; namely, the take-off and landing. These elements are basic for all aircraft but the handling and speeds vary considerably.

Take-off

To assist this action, the runway is selected to give the nearest position to flying directly into the wind. For modern giant beasts, this is not of vital importance, but most WWII planes would behave better for what assistance a head wind could give the pilot. A strong cross-wind is not pleasant for our pilot; hence most UK airfields were built with three runways which usually avoided any wind blowing at say 90 degrees to the runway.

We are now at the end of the correct runway, so we now push throttle(s) fully forward to give maximum power. We then gather speed and with most wartime RAF planes the third wheel is to the rear (some US models had nose wheels). In the case of our Cark Ansons we have rumbled over half the runway and will be over 70 mph. Then we feel the rear end lift off the runway and with experience we feel the right moment to ease back control and start climbing to say 1,000 feet. We can then reduce power and fly horizontally, or climb gradually to operating height. We have also operated the undercarriage to raise wheels.

The Anson has no vices and there is nothing dramatic in our take-offs, however this is not the case for all types. Some can swerve off the runway or require huge distance before a climb can be commenced. If, however, the engine or one engine in our Anson fails, we have a very hasty situation - usually a disastrous crash. Most twin engine aircraft will fly level on one engine, albeit hard work for the pilot on wartime models. Four engine types can cope easily on three motors.

Landing

This is in most cases more difficult than take-off. The War's single engine machines force the pilot to look 'over the side' when approaching the runway, whereas multi-engine models usually have good visibility over the nose. As remarked before, the lack of a nose wheel requires the pilot to attempt a three-point landing (two landing wheels plus tail wheel). The word "attempt" is quite apt as it is extremely difficult to arrive at such perfection.

The reverse of our take-off procedures is fairly obvious, wheels are lowered, the locking is checked and then turn to line-up with the selected runway. Throttle reduced and approach speed adjusted, approximately 80 mph for our Anson (much faster for most fighters). With experience the pilot will aim to touch-down in the one third runway area nearest to the perimeter. This gave plenty of room to slow and avoid excessive braking, or worse, to crash off the end of the runway.

Our Anson is a delight to land. With a little power the final action is akin to a 'lift' and a final ease back on the control and hey presto, a perfect (or near enough) 'three pointer' is accomplished! It's nothing like as easy in a

Spitfire, Hurricane or heavy bombers, especially a Wellington. The Spitfire has a narrow undercarriage, so if wings are not steady and parallel with the field, the landing could result in a violent lurch with a possible wing tip hitting the ground.

Heavy landing with any aircraft can be disastrous, or at least result in a burst tyre or damaged undercarriage. Night landings are several degrees more difficult than daylight. Heavy rain is trying especially for the single engine types.

Instruments

Four instruments were vital: air speed indicator, artificial horizon, altimeter and compass. The artificial horizon was a brilliant piece of innovation, the sensitive diagram shows every movement of the wings in relation to the ground (you know instantly if you are flying level, diving or climbing). Night flying, or flying in clouds would be impossible without this device. The altimeter is a barometer; the thinner higher air with differing air pressure is converted into feet (or metres). The compass was a standard, approximately six inches in diameter; very clear and reliable.Further instruments were mostly concerned with engine performance: Revs Per Minute, boost, oil pressure and of course the fuel gauge. As the aircraft models became larger and more refined, such as a Lancaster bomber with four engines, the array of dials became quite a collection for one pilot to assimilate.

Link trainer

This was a wartime boon; a very clever aid to flying 'blind'. The pupil sat in a mock-up cockpit and a hood covered the seat area to produce total darkness. A simulated instrument panel was in front of the 'pilot' plus compass and control stick. The supervisor outside gave instructions as to course and speed etc. The simulated controls were very sensitive and not easy. The result of maybe 30 minutes was shown to the instructor as a graph. Every error was clearly visible! Many pupils hated the *@?*!* Link. A common expression was "Stuff the *@?*!* missing link!"

Maintenance

The system of maintenance for aircraft is based on hours flown. The crew specialise on engines, airframe, instruments and son on. Bear in mind thousands of young men and women had to be trained very quickly in a field, which in most cases was completely foreign to their civilian occupations. At Cark the quality of maintenance was very good. The C/O W/C Gibb was keen to have a reliable team and very often he would have a brief chat with the Service Officer during the midday lunch break in the Officers' Mess.

In many theatres of the war the RAF ground staff performed miracles: in Malta; in the N African desert conditions; in tropical rain in Burma and on flying boat bases ground crews were required to work from the harbour or water base. Huge numbers of the RR Merlin engines were fitted to fighters and four engine bombers. These engines were very complicated pieces of rather delicate machinery, but had to be checked and often removed and replaced by a new motor - and quickly. Too little praise has been allotted to these gallant hard working airmen and airwomen, who all helped to keep thousands of hard used aircraft flying all over the world.

Survival

One military historian graphically outlined the possibilities of a RAF Spitfire pilot surviving in a squadron engaged with interception fighting in 1940. The factors involved include: an above average flying ability, preferably exceptional ability; excellent eyesight; many hours of training on Spitfires; having a good seasoned Squadron Commander and a 'good shooting eye' to operate the fighters' guns to the most lethal. Then we have factors beyond the choice or ability of the pilot. These imply the need for an aircraft superior to the enemy: the squadron(s) to be superior in numbers to that of the enemy; excellent radar ground force information; a wide undercarriage to assist landing on a bumpy field (in case of no runways); good meteorological information; first class maintenance crews to avoid engine or structural failure and above all LUCK and more LUCK! Considering this very thorough analysis, it is amazing that any of our heroic 'few' survived at all!

Aircraft survival

Very little analysis has been exposed for public reading concerning the 'lost' aircraft. By this we can ponder over the fact that far more aircraft were produced than the number lost in front-line operations. One example is the total production of Hurricanes was about 15,000; this is far beyond the number destroyed in action. This shows the huge number damaged beyond repair in accidents: lost in transit; damage from storms, fire and so on. Even in 1940 our production of Spitfires and Hurricanes was more than replacing operational losses. Of course our aircrew, especially pilots, were injured or died in many accidents not connected with combat duties. On this rather sombre note we can safely say there is more to handling and maintaining aircraft than driving a Ford Fiesta up the M6!

Elementary theory of dead reckoning navigation

The navigation in the air is virtually the same principle as for the mariners. The big difference however, is the relative slow speed of the ship. This infers that the calculations in the air have to be as quick as possible. Even the modest speeds of WWII bombers could be near to five miles per minute – ten times faster than a ship.

If we could fly in a wind-free atmosphere, we would not require any navigation refinements. Like sea currents and tides, the wind can blow us well off course. In the early days of the war, the Luftwaffe arrived over our cities without any unit navigation. They flew from France, a short distance to London or the south coast airfields or ports following a radio beam. A young British scientist interested Churchill in his theories. He was granted research funds and fortunately, the RAF technicians neutered the beam. So much so, on one raid a German landed near Dover assuming he was over France. This scientist saved thousands of British lives. The RAF copied this system which would reach Rhineland with great effect. Of course the Germans learned our frequencies and like the Germans, we had to disband the concept.

Astro-navigation was used extensively on ships. Bearings on stars and the sun could often be taken fairly accurately if sea was not rough and in up to maybe fifteen minutes, a good fix (position) could be achieved. Although tuition was given in advanced RAF navigation courses, it was rarely used and exceedingly difficult.

Hence the 'Dead Reckoning' system was used. We have to find fixes by any means possible. The ideal method is to note a landmark very close to our track, or underneath it. By noting exact time, we then have the ideal situation – we know where we are at 'x' hours. To add to an accurate fix, if we know the precise wind speed and direction, we can calculate by trigonometry a good estimate of where we will be in say, the next hour's duration.

Unfortunately navigation needs some intuition and 'guessology'. For example, we always know our ground wind speed and direction very accurately at the site of our initial take-off (by anemometer etc). At say 8,000 feet the speed will increase by at least 10%. Also due to friction at ground level, the direction will be at least 10% different because of earth's rotational speed. So before we leave the runway, we have to adjust details of the ground wind. Next, if our destination is say 200 miles in W Europe, the wind details will certainly be different from our guessed initial wind. By studying meteorological information (if we have them) we can use this knowledge to improve our future guess. Additionally, en route we will probably have to alter course and adjust our estimated time of arrival (ETA).

Let me use a simple example. The wind is west 270 degrees; point A to point B is 150 miles. With the information of track direction, wind speed and direction, we can find the angle to give us the correct course. This calculation is obtained in a minute from a vital circular calculator (about four inches in diameter). About 100 miles en route we plot a landmark for an accurate fix. This gives us a revised track, course and ETA.

This process is repeated for the final journey. This shows the ability to obtain fixes is essential for very accurate navigation. So the reader can understand the extreme difficulties in navigating at night over Germany. Hence the squadrons of the highly skilled and brave Pathfinders group were formed.

Our views from the cockpit

The best view from almost every aircraft is from the cockpit with a good arc in front and below. Most of our pilots were trained in Canada or Africa; areas which are featureless for hundreds of miles. The Prairie winter offers the pilots with (mostly) sunshine and a sea of white to the horizon. Africa delivers most of the year, a yellowish or brown plain and masses of sunshine.

The early days at Cark must have been quite a shock for any Staff Pilot, with hills almost on the end of two runways and another above Grange-over-Sands. The routes, although traversing over a lot of sea, passed over and near coastal landmarks. We had green on the hillsides and fields for twelve months of the year. Despite this variety and vastly more 'intimate' landscapes, most of the pilots became bored with the view and some never accepted the job as essential for safety and accuracy for our pupils.

It is probably a true saying, "That beauty is in the eyes of the beholder". Nevertheless, the range of landscapes when flying from Cark is distinct and very attractive. The most contrasting would be a flawless, calm, frosty day in January, flying at maybe 6,000 feet above The Lakes; snow-capped mountains and Skiddaw to Ingleborough all in view and reflections off all the major lakes, a sight never to be forgotten. Compare this with low cloud pushing the Ansons down to about 3,000 feet, gusty rain causing the plane to buck and shudder, straight ahead the yellow sand of Walney Island and the white streak of the surf crashing home!

The immediate area close to the airfield has a maze of detail: Flookburgh village on the perimeter; Grange a spit away; Holder Hall estate with superb trees and lush meadows; the complex estuary of the Kent (plus viaduct); the River Leven and Arnside Knott.

Flying north from Walney, we have the Cumbrian west coast on our starboard. No Sellafield scar had been inscribed in the landscape at this time. The most westerly point is St Bees Head with red sandstone cliffs. The Whitehaven harbour is also a good landmark. Across the Solway estuary are green fields, farms and a few villages. Flying west we come to the Mull of Galloway, a granite finger with savage looking cliffs pushing into the north Irish Sea. On the Mull itself are sub-tropical gardens, almost (but not quite!) rivalling Tresco the Prince of Wales' garden de luxe in the Scillies.

Some routes took us across the Irish side of the sea. The mountains of Munroe do come down to the sea. They have their own character, not craggy like Scafell or the Langdale Pikes, but dark and forbidding with sculptured smooth flowing lines to the beaches below. A very different view is flying toward and along the north shore of Anglesey. Form 5,000 feet the size and shape of the island is plain to grasp. The most scenic spot are the massive granite sea cliffs in the Holyhead area. Usually there's plenty of white surf with the crashing waves. In a few minutes we'd pass parallel with the superb curving beach of Llandudno.

A huge W-E runway was built near Valley. This was to assist US bombers (Flying Fortresses) to land safely after crossing the Atlantic. Today it is home to fighter-bombers flying at over 1,000 mph.

Flying Fortress

We usually turned northerly at this point and a route could pick up the sand dunes at Birkdale; then across the Ribble estuary to pin point over Blackpool Tower. It looks like a rusty piece of Meccano from our flying height. Another few minutes and Heysham to Morcambe is in sight. A good pin point could be the open air Baths, especially if it had water to reflect any sunshine.

The Isle of Man was our favourite spot to give the pupils opportunity to use either the north (Point of Ayre) or the southerly extremity (Calf of Man) for a precise fix. From about fifteen miles the whole outline of the Island could easily be recognised. There was a good sized airfield at Jurby in the NW. Another RAF Training Command Station with Ansons in use. The Calf of Man was our favourite due to its small complex cliffs and separation from the SE corner of the mainland. There were always white splurges of surf, easily visible even in poor conditions.

Then home across the last leg to our well-loved Walney Island! The sandy stretch of N-S beach was as good as a radio beacon or lit lighthouse. A few minutes of descending flying east up the narrowing estuary readied us to join the Cark circuit at 1,000 feet. About seven times out of ten we then flew over Humphrey to land on one of the runways pointing to the west. No one can say we did not have endless variety of views and weather – a long way from the Prairies of Veld!

Mountain frolics and fatalities

A very unusual duty assigned to RAF Cark was the maintenance of two valuable safety devices. On the summit of Skiddaw and Helvellyn were radio signal transmitters. They were powered by old fashioned batteries which were very heavy and bulky. They fitted on to fairly crude wooden frames. We had volunteers to carry these loads, with a usual three or four man crew. In winter we tried to use a four man system to give more relief to the 'Sherpas' and extra safety in case of any accident.

We had no disasters, but many winter ascents had snow, mist and gales etc to hamper their progress. We used a three ton truck with a WAAF driver to transport this crew to suitable bases. The RAF had no rule system to kit them out with adequate clothing. Most of the volunteers were fell walkers or rock climbers so they used their togs of choice. This practice seems typical with the reports we have seen regarding our army troops in Iraq and Afghanistan! We tried to improve frames but we could not alter the rectangular shape or size. Before the days of urethane foam, we tried various padding systems to fit under the shoulder straps.

In 1942 with momentum and two Jeeps 'organised' by W/C Gibb (C/O), we soon had a nucleus of four rock climbers including 'Scotty' Dwyer with his experience on Scottish mountains. A colourful volunteer was a burly (ex rugger) Sgt Staff Pilot. His nickname was 'Tiger', partly due to his handling the left hand drive Jeeps and his appearance. He had a mop of curly red hair matched with a bushy moustache. He was hailed as a hero and plied with free beer when he worked out a tortuous route up the lower slopes of Skiddaw and one day he reached the 1,000 foot level! There was little scope for adventure in the lower reaches of Helvellyn to the chagrin of the climbers! Fortunately he failed to overturn a Jeep to our relief.

We set up regular training sessions, which usually developed into two pairs tackling rock routes on Dow Crags, Gimmer Crag, Langdale, Bowfell Buttress, Castle Rock, Thirlmere and a few smaller ones near the valley bottom in Langdale. Our personal successes involved the second ascent of a hard climb on Castle Rock. This route had been made a few weeks previously by Jim Birkett of Langdale. He was at the time the number one rock climber since 1938. Later we made our own first ascent on the steep shapely South Buttress of Dow Crags. We had no fancy gear in those days; hemp rope and F W Woolworth plimsolls!

The term 'rescue' was unfortunately never factual. Any crashes on the rocky hill areas involved massive destruction of the aircraft and a sudden end for the crew. In some areas of the Pennine and the periphery of the lakes, peaty, boggy conditions prevailed. An aircraft could bury deeply in such places. For most of the war years the farms had limited labour and very few ramblers walked over strange routes. In some accidents the remains were traced years after the initial tragedy.

We experienced one ghastly call-out. It was a Saturday in winter. We had a call about mid-afternoon and we had difficulty in mustering a crew. I hijacked my good friend F/Lt Dean and 'Tiger' volunteered to drive one Jeep. It was raining hard, so with canvas roofs in the 'up' position we set off with a small amount of food and rubber capes.

The destination was a remote farm some miles into the hills in the Kirkby Stephen area. We had no one inch Ordnance Survey map, so we had to find the farm by asking the nearest habitation. By the time we found the farm, it was dark, and we only had four torches between our motley gang. The farmer gave us his version of position.

He ignored the fact that we had never seen his sheep farm in daylight. After an hour in the now increasing gale, we saw a glint in our feeble torch beam. As we approached this object it was clear that we were looking at part of a tail fin of a Halifax Bomber. We struggled round the area for another hour and could find only small parts of a wing or fuselage. We came to the conclusion it had crashed some years previously and nine tenths of it was buried in the hill bog.

The Jeep headlamps were masked with just narrow slits giving a modicum of light. The trip back was a nightmare, due to visibility reducing us to about 15 mph and various stops to check a junction en route. We were very thankful that our Jeeps were left hand drive as this enabled us to follow hedges and side fences as they were often only inches away!

The massive crash on the fells above Little Langdale was a horrible sight. A large bomber pulverised into the gully and mountain outcrops of granite. The Air Force sent a Corporal mechanic and his assistant. They stayed in the local pub and eventually informed their station that any worthwhile salvage was well beyond their miniscule efforts.

Many years after the War's end, a historian author published a thin book listing air accidents in Cumbria. He had traced over one hundred accidents. Most of this horrific number was not surprisingly, in the ten year period from 1938 to 1948.

The northern sector of the county seemed to have been the worst sector. One airfield in Silloth was used to train Coastal Command pilots on twin engine Hudsons. This aircraft was a US plane and difficult to fly. The maintenance may also be involved, being a non-British made model. A macabre nickname emanated from Silloth. The Solway Firth was a graveyard for a number of crashes, so the Solway was re-christened as 'Hudson Bay'. The weirdest of crashes was when <u>three</u> Ansons in loose formation leaving an airfield outside Cumbria crashed into the northern fells.

Lockheed Hudson

Some local characters or "up the khyber"!

Many readers may not realise the social mix was rather extreme in the swathe of territory from Grange to Ambleside in 1939. Pre WWI the situation was almost 'rich or poor'.

Our C/O (W/C Gibb) was welcomed by some of the 'gentry' where he enjoyed shooting and salmon fishing. He received a variety of invitations, especially for afternoon tea on Sundays. He passed these on to our Medical Officer ('Doc') who would be socially accepted by most of these locals. The 'Doc' accepted a few and for reinforcement persuaded two or three officers to join him for the experience.

I enjoyed four of these strange jaunts. They were good representatives of the strands of wealth and social class at that time. Most of the wealth emanated from mill owning families from West Yorkshire or Lancashire textiles, colonial offices, or retired mid to high ranking officers from the Services. My section covers this analysis.

The most 'normal' and very engaging was an ex Attorney General of Uganda, Sir Thomas Tomlinson who had a fine old house a few miles north of Grange. His house was like an African museum! He had a great sense of humour and gave us a very good insight into the tribal labyrinth of the East African colonies. He expected most of the area would make efforts (or warfare) to extract independence from Britain after the War's end. He also expected massive upheaval and poor government. How true he was!

A very different 'local' had a nickname of 'Sinbad'! He lived near Cartmel in a Victorian house. The sizeable front garden had an uncut lawn lined with untrimmed shrubs. Half buried in the deep grass was a large dinghy, keel uppermost. Almost out of sight were oars, lanterns, coils of rope, poles and lobster posts!

This mariner was a retired Sales Director of a family woollen mill near Bradford. The mill was flat out, producing the low grade Battledress fabrics in three colours. He liked the Cartmel valley as he could catch a train heading for Yorkshire. He went to board meetings four to six times a year.

He had a huge lounge with a massive bay window. In one corner was a large steel safe. As soon as we arrived he produced malt whisky and the 'correct' style of glasses. Apparently he travelled widely from about 1910 to 1935 and displayed his old passports. A very impressive list of countries showed their stamps. The collection included Russia, Japan, most of Europe and some British colonies in Africa.

After he downed a few 'refreshers', he waxed in full spate and told us about his two boys ensconced in Sedbergh School and how he visited Harrods four times a year, to buy presents and a stock of hats for his wife. He added that she only wore some once, so they burned these on November 5th! The weirdest piece of legerdemain was when he produced a mass of bank pass books. Some were in his name and many in his wife's name. It seems he did not trust the banks overmuch, so if one or two folded he had a dozen or so left intact! The deposits varied from £2,000 to £20,000.

His nickname was earned when he first moved to Cumbria and hired some of the Flookburgh fishermen to assist him to collect yachts when he made purchases. Some were bought in the Isle of Wight and had to be sailed to Arnside. His sailings also included shipping the boats to buyers. His favourite trip was from Oban to Dublin in a heavy gale.

The 'Doc' was very enthusiastic about another of 'Gibbo's' cast offs. We had an invite to visit a retired Indian Army Surgeon. This man lived singly, an elderly bachelor who had a superb house on the hillside above Grasmere. He had a massive window with panoramic views across the lake. In this room he had a massive library.

The books were mostly leather bound, with a fine collection of Indian history. He was in his element discussing medical matters with 'Doc' who was about thirty-five years his junior. The old army survivor had served at least thirty years in the service and had visited many areas and army stations including the notorious 'NW Frontier'. The enemy were Pushtoons or Afghans.

He expected India to seek independence very soon and could not see how a unified government would cope with the castes, tribes and schism between Muslims and Hindus. He had a live-in gardener cum chauffer and his cook. He enjoyed our company and was almost 'fluent' in navigation before we left!

Another fascinating 'local' lived in an old solid looking stone house near Newby Bridge. A very large garden had two large glasshouses. They were used for intensive tomato growing and a smaller number of beans and peppers. Another Empire servant, he had obtained a language degree from Cambridge. After some European posting in the Foreign Office service, he was promoted to a District Officer in Burma and subsequently served nearly twenty years in Malay. He often made two or three week 'tours' by boat and horse to legislate against disputes in the more remote areas. He usually had a Malay NCO and six or eight armed native troops for protection. He was awarded an OBE for this work.

His father was a very wealthy lawyer and landowner based in Barrow and West Cumbria. He had two brothers and a sister. They all had public school and university education. One brother was an architect and civil engineering adviser to the Colonial Office; he was involved in harbour building in Singapore. His other brother was a medical officer in Burma, stationed with his wife, also a qualified medical doctor. His sister had a literature degree from Cambridge, never married and 'kept home' for her parents.

Our local ex administrator's pride and joy was his large dining room. This had oak panels on the walls, a massive oak table and eight chairs to match. He claimed the panels had been removed from one of Oliver Cromwell's houses. His second indulgence was his glasshouses and products! Our host urged us to return any weekend. He estimated a load of tomatoes would be ready for picking in less than three weeks, when we were welcome to take them for the Officers' Mess!

Three years previous to our meeting his wife had died. He was very bitter with the British Army as he knew his only son had been taken prisoner by the Japanese in the debacle and surrender of Singapore. Like him, his son was also a Colonial Officer in Malay and had 'escaped' to Singapore. He also hoped the RAF could develop bases and equipment to bomb mainland Japan as soon as possible.

I believe most or all of the family died off prior to 1960; a truly fine family who were the best types of Empire builders. A pity the Empire critics could not have met many of the educated Brits. Those who spent most of their lives developing a veneer of civilisation in numerous territories and may never have lived sufficiently long enough to enjoy any retirement back 'home'.

Due to 'Gibbo's' PR expertise, we surprisingly had two very interesting visitors to the Mess. Firstly, we had more than one evening with W Heaton Cooper, the famous Grasmere watercolour artist. He showed some of his work and gave us a short talk. The other visit was also an artist, but very different. He was a retired cartoonist for one of the Manchester newspapers. He made a couple of pencil portraits and gave an insight into his work and deadlines.

Anecdotes from cark

A night flight had on board two navigational trainers and a navigation instructor. The pilot was a new Staff Pilot. On the completion of an accurate tour of the Irish Sea area, the pilot was using a green light signal to guide him on to the W-E runway. The instructor suddenly realised the Anson was heading for Carnforth Railway Station! Full throttle and a rapid climb saved the situation!

A US Liberator bomber asked for an urgent landing. The crew had flown from Canada and missed Anglesey. We advised them to proceed to Walney RAF. The pilot said he was worried about fuel shortage. After a trial circuit, the pilot made a superb approach and landing. With red hot brakes he came to a juddering stop on the Flookburgh shrimp fisherman's road, with the nose hovering over the adjacent drain ditch! After a good night's rest and food the take-off was almost as nerve shredding as the landing. An hour later he landed in one piece at the huge US base at Burtonwood near Warrington.

Not as fortunate as the American crew, a RAF Wellington two engine bomber landed wheels up on the sands at low tide. He missed anti-invasion poles but the aircraft had to be dismantled - a long and weary job!

The following event occurred before my 'watch' but was told by a reliable Cark Officer: A night flight was on the last leg from N Ireland to Cark. The route was planned to fly to the Calf of Man, an islet on the south tip at 5,000 feet. On board were a Staff Pilot and two Australian trainees. For some reason or gross error, the plane was well below the safe height and grazed the top peaty slopes of Snaefell, the highest point of the Isle of Man. By a miracle the crew survived serious injury and using the axe cut out from the fuselage into inky darkness! After a struggle and mishaps they spotted a small light, which eventually proved to be a farmer's cottage. The occupant had no phone, so it was daybreak before the farmer could cycle to the nearest police station. From this, they were collected by RAF Jurby, a training air station. The following day they were ferried back to Cark!

Dating and mating

As the War progressed it is widely accepted that the social and sexual norm of pre 1940 rapidly changed or many people believed, were eroded. The eventual promiscuity was quite understandable with the huge upheaval of family life and the concentration of young men and women on airfields and army camps.

The worst by-product of this social breakdown was unwanted pregnancies. Possibly due to the high quality of our WAAF officers, we had no epidemic among the Cark WAAFs.

The ground staff, although mostly male had a fair opportunity of making friends with the WAAF contingency, which may have limited the need to mix with the local young women. Outside the camp dances in the village halls were common place and usually crowded. The RAF had an advantage over the Army on the dance floor; the RAF wore shoes, whereas the army lads had to crunch round in boots!

A modest number of the local girls were forced out of circulation. This was the development of a small factory in Ulverston where aircraft components had to be cleaned down with paraffin baths. The girls worked shifts and most detested the job. Some were sorry they had not joined the services!

There was one lonesome Land Army girl who worked hard on a farm near Cartmel. She sometimes had a break at weekends. We felt sorry for her and urged her to try for a transfer to the RAF.

Not many relationships matured into marriage. Two couples were notable. We have mentioned previously the sad outcome of our 'Queen Bee' who married a Polish Staff Pilot who was sadly killed during bombing. Another happier case was one of our Staff Pilots nicknamed 'Timber'; his surname was probably Wood! He was a quiet unassuming man and possibly slightly introspective. He was no 'oil painting' and looked older than his true age. He was however always well groomed and his shoes could advertise Cherry Blossom!

We had from time to time visitors' day and on such occasion 'Timber' brought his new girl-friend. We were bowled over. His companion looked not more than twenty, tall, slender and very pretty. She had the unusual combination of dense black wavy hair and vivid intense blue eyes. 'Timber' was bombarded with questions: How had he 'pulled' the prettiest girl in Kendal? They soon married and set up home soon after the War in S Lancashire where 'Timber' could really earn his nickname and became a woodwork teacher!

A Cartmel clanger

The King's Arms, Cartmel was packed with Cark personnel and a few locals like most Saturday nights. In the smoke screen melee was a Wing Commander who was visiting the airfield. Sitting in one corner were two WAAFs. A F/O standing next to the 'Winco' leaned over towards the girls and pointing to his three rings on his sleeve asked if they could move to make sitting room.

One of the girls had imbibed in 'one too many' and in a loud voice exclaimed, "I don't care if he has rings from his arse to his elbow, I'm not budging!" The 'Winco' thought this was the highlight of the evening!

The 'ard 'ard 'ammer of the 'orses 'ooves on the 'ard 'ard road

Some of the sleeping quarters were set parallel to the straight, narrow, paved road leading from Flookburgh Square to the shore. The shrimp fishermen used horse and carts. They worked in all weathers and had to harmonise with the tides. Unfortunately the clop, clop of the heavy horses gait often woke us. Some nights we had to suffer a convoy of three carts in succession. However, we accepted they were helping to feed the country and it was a very arduous job and not without danger. Also, some of their young men had joined the Royal Navy.

Completely squashed

One of the many virtues of life at RAF Cark was the available squash courts. This was my first opportunity to play regularly. My roommate Ray Dean was like me, a tyro, so we could easily fit in three or four sessions per week.

One day after lunch the 'Queen Bee' approached me and exclaimed, "I say Parky old boy, can you fit in a squash game around four o'clock?" I could not refuse the lady and duly reported at the court at 16:00 hours prompt.

We now draw a veil over the session. In five games I failed to extract one point! I had not been warned that her ladyship had played at her public school from eleven to eighteen. Then at university she played in the varsity team and had fairly often played near her home! Being a man I was sweating profusely, but my opponent, a true lady, was merely flushed!

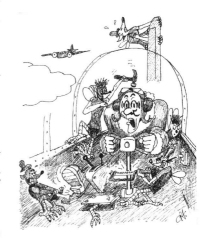

A Cark of a day

The RAF more so than either the Army or Navy, concocted many colourful slang phrases. One which has lasted is 'Gremlin'. Probably the most zany is 'Wizard Prang'. This was most apt in the grim days of 1940 when many young pilots had to make belly landings on the grassy airfields due to a shot-up undercarriage.

166

At RAF Cark we did our bit in this area of linguistic innovation. Around 08:00 hours struggling against a gusty wind and rain, cycling to the Control Tower (all of twenty feet away), we would eventually climb the steps to be greeted by a ginning meteorological girl. She would show the Navigation Officer on duty a horrible mass of isobars and a thick pencil line denoting the depression front pushing east over the Irish Sea,

"All seagulls grounded!"

The Navigation Officer would reply, "Another Cark of a day!"

Nothing but a hound dog

One perfect early summer evening, our Mountain Rescue jeep with four on board came to a full stop on the top of the steep road leading to Lindale village. We had a married officer in our crew and were to drop him off at his rented cottage to be welcomed by his wife. A few vehicles were stopped in front, so we ambled down the hill to expect an accident.

To our amazement we found one of the locals holding up the traffic. Then we heard the howls of fell hounds. They were following an aniseed trail on the nearby hills. The route was to take them over the road and a further three miles to Cartmel Racecourse field!

The whip hand

The railways during the War were a lifeline carrying passengers, many of which were armed services and also vital freight. Delays of one to several hours were common due to breakdowns, labour shortage and minor accidents. In the Cark saga, the most famous train was the last evening train from Carnforth to Barrow. This was given the bizarre nickname of 'The

Whip'. It was said to ship in the stragglers getting back to Cark from leave, or at weekends from Morecambe or Blackpool.

One Saturday when our Navigation Department was four strong, we decided for some barmy reason to train it across the bay to Arnside for a dance. This trip was on time and we soon found the crowded small village hall. Around 22:30 hours we decided to head for the station in case 'The Whip' was on time. Two hours later we all agreed 'The Whip' was NOT on time! Now the foursome had two choices: one, to sit it out and wait, or two, hike across the railway bridge to Cark perimeter!

Yes, you guessed right! Four weary navigators started plodding from 'sleeper' to 'sleeper', cursing and stumbling. The night was pitch black and we did not rise with Cark on the Sunday morning – so the railway had 'The Whip Hand'.

"The hypocritic oath!"

Our Cark Medical Officer was a great guy; quite young and dedicated to every aspect of his varied responsibilities. Although he used the Officer's Mess, he did not booze or mix much with the younger pilot mob. He made use of his limited spare time studying hard for his aspiration to become a member of the College of Surgeons. He found the examination very difficult, especially as 'Doc' had no experienced hospital medicos to confer with on a daily basis.

One week we urged him to have a leisure day, when we would introduce him to a Lakeland mountain and if he trusted us, we would steer him up a crag. We picked a perfect summer's day and selected Langdale. Bowfell Buttress looked tempting. About six of us sweated up the Band, a track up from the head of the valley towards the top ridges. 'Doc' was not over enthusiastic when he looked up the three hundred feet or so to the Buttress. After a rest and a good gulp of water, 'Scotty' Dwyer roped up and had 'Doc' as number two in a three up team. An 'easy' route was used and the Doctor, who was tall, lean and fit, did well for the first fifty feet.

He then came up to a fairly steep wall of twenty feet and a lovely stream of invectives streamed across the mountain air, "How the *@?*!* hell do I get up this, you b******s?"

The number three climber shouted up to 'Doc', "Is that what you call a hypocritical oath?"

He enjoyed his day's exertions and agreed it was a real change from pouring over anatomy, or the mysteries of pharmacology!

"The Mull of bloody Galloway"

In one of the rare weeks in summer when we had 'wall to wall' sunshine and light winds we tried to cram in four daytime flights. On the Friday we decided to give the pupils some overland delights, so the first leg was Cark to Carlisle. We flew at 6,000 feet, so if a single engine failed the Staff Pilot could turn back and re-trim the Anson. This allowed for a loss of 1,000 feet, giving 2,000 feet of spare over the highest Lakes peaks..

"THAT'S THE BLOODY MULL OF GALAWAY!"

The second leg was turning westerly, descending to 5,000 feet and then set a course arriving to pass the south tip of the Mull of Galloway about two miles offshore. Trust the Irish Sea microclimate to spoil our plans. The crews found that a sheet of low stratus was covering a fair area of the Solway Firth.

One crew ordered their pilot to descend and break through the cloud. The pilot followed their instruction and was around 500 or 600 feet over the open sea when breaking cloud. Up to one mile ahead were the granite cliffs of the Mull. One of the pupils was wide awake and slapped the pilot on his head and shouted, "Left hand down, full throttle, that's the bloody Mull of Galloway!"

The Staff Pilot was probably at fault, two or three degrees off his correct course and should have descended more steeply to break cover at least five miles from the Mull. The other crews had no problems.

And finally a real 'cough drop'!

To understand this aptus verbum we should explain that all services in the War years had in their surgeries a large bottle on a shelf. The label on this bottle had the intriguing inscription, "MISTIC.SPEC". Non Latin scholars guessed this may have been an abbreviation for something like 'misticus specialis' or special mixture. In fact, this concoction was a typical cough medicine of the time.

Some of the airmen's sleeping huts had a flat roof porch over the entrance. During off duty hours, one of the mechanics had a weird whim to sit cross-legged on a cushion on top of his porch. He was a great reader and with his jet black hair and thick black rimmed spectacles he always looked studious. Apparently on some days he had a well-worn tome, which was a biography of Saint Thomas Aquias, the BC religious philosopher!

A few of us were having some 'crack' in the Officers' Mess and one officer mentioned this odd bod and asked if anyone else had noticed his very bizarre appearance and leisure time occupation.

"Oh Yes," said one of the group, "he's a real cough drop!"

"No" exclaimed another officer, "I am sure he is the original MISTIC SPEC!"

G F Parkinson

(2011)

170

Mr C Richardson – Cark 1944

I was stationed at Cark from the 30th of July 1944 until the 29th of August. I am afraid that I have no photographs from my time there and can recall little of my course except for a very unusual bombing incident which happened like this:

On the 4th of August 1944 I took off as Pilot with F/Sgt Nicholls, an Australian, to carry out a practice bombing of the target in Morcambe Bay which to my recollection was just off the Carnforth coast. Upon reaching the target F/Sgt Nicholls got into the nose where the bombsight was located and I opened the bomb doors and watched the 'tell tales' emerge indicating that the bomb doors were open. We made our first run. Nicholls called out "bombs gone" and then, "sorry skipper I've not seen that one". We made another run with the same result.

I now suspected there was something wrong, aborted the exercise, pulled the aircraft into a steep turn and headed back to base landing 'on tiptoe'. On landing I got hold of an armament fitter and told him the tale. He promptly got under the aircraft and pulled open the doors. Much to my surprise nothing fell out and there were no 'hang ups'. Where were the missing bombs?

Unknown to me the chain drive which opened the bomb doors was broken but there was enough left on the sprocket to work the 'tell tales' without opening the doors. A few minutes later I was called to Flying Control to be told that two bombs had fallen on Carnforth! Fortunately they had fallen

Chap here wants a word about that 'hang-up' you managed to shake loose!

between two houses without doing any damage. It appears that when I made the steep turn centrifugal force had taken over and the bombs had sprung together again after the bombs had gone.

It cost me five shillings in the Red Cross box to forget the incident. I thought this was a bit unfair at the time since it was hardly my fault but I paid up without a murmur just to make a quick exit from Flying Control and forget the whole thing. There were never any repercussions for which I was grateful.

We then climbed into another Anson and completed the exercise. So it's very strange that I have come back to live so close to the scene of my escapade since I came from the North East of England originally and spent all my working life in Bolton, Lancashire.

You can be sure I have made no enquiries since coming to live in the Carnforth area!

Mr C Richardson 2011

Mr L White – RAF Cark 1943

I arrived late in 1943 to take a radio operators course before going on to an Operational Training Unit prior to joining my bomber squadron down in Lincolnshire. By the end of the War I simply wanted to forget about my experiences and so when I was offered the chance to apply for my flying log book I declined the opportunity. Because of this my course date at Cark is only a guess but I believe it began in November and lasted about three or four weeks. We trained in a special 'wireless room' and in the air. I was not a natural airman to begin with and suffered a great deal with airsickness but by the time I arrived at Cark I was almost over that which was as well because the routes we took on the several flights I endured as part of my course involved a rough ride in the turbulent air above the Lakeland hills.

Of the area, I recall the local fishermen; their horses pulling cars piled with nets as they made their way to the sands and the village pubs that always offered a warm welcome and good beer.

Cark Anson - photo L.White

Mr L White 1996

Mr F. W. Ramsay — 1942/43

At the beginning of 1942, Training Command were unable to get what were termed as "Screened Aircrew". This meant aircrew who had completed a tour of operations and were due to be rested. These crews were being kept at Operational Training Units etc which came under Bomber Command, so

W/ops course Cark 1943
front right W/Off Fred Ramsay

Training Command decided to train their own Staff Crews. In June 1942 I was one of 21 Wireless Operators who were posted in to RAF Millom. Being a Fleetwood lad this was a good posting for me as I was able to go home on my days off. Once we had passed our Air Operating Course at Millom we did a month's Gunnery Training at RAF Walney. I enjoyed this a great deal. We trained on the Boulton Paul Defiant Aircraft and after passing out with "Wings and Stripes" at the end of July 1942 I returned to RAF Millom to join the stations staff.

I was married whilst serving at Millom on the 19th December 1942. With my aircrew leave and days off I spent a happy Christmas at home, but was feeling a bit fed up as I caught the last train back to Millom. I was even more fed up when I was told that I had been posted to RAF Wigtown with effect from the next morning! I was only at Wigtown two months when they opened a new station to train, Staff Pilots at RAF Cark. I can honestly say that I enjoyed every minute of my stay at Cark. I was posted there as a SGT and left as a Warrant Officer for an Operational Training Unit. From O.T.U. I was eventually crewed up and we were posted to RAF Luffenham for training on the four engine heavy Lancaster Bombers. As we finished our course, VE Day was declared, Bomber Command found themselves redundant and that was the last of

Electrical section Cark
photo Fred Ramsay

my flying. I was posted to RAF Kirkham (now Kirkham Prison) for an equipment assistants course which I completed before being de-mobbed in March 1946.

Fred Ramsay 1992

CHAPTER 3

Relics and Reminders
Items of historical interest still around today

Cark Airfield stands today as one of the finest surviving examples of a WWII 'expansion period' installation in the North West of England. This is due largely to continued and varied usage of its infrastructure over the years. Presented here is a selection of photographs which illustrate and identify artefacts and architectural features associated with RAF Cark which survive to the present day.

The 20mm cannon shells shown in the photo on the right are somewhat of an enigma as no heavy cannon equipped aircraft operated from RAF Cark to the best of my knowledge. These items were found adjacent to the machine gun range in 1962 and my only supposition could be that when the Hurricane Mk IV fighter aircraft were brought to RAF Cark for target towing duties they came equipped with heavy cannon which would probably subsequently have been removed. The true reason for the existence of these shells on the range remains a mystery which is further compounded by the fact that two of the shells show no sign of having been fired.

Cark's machine gun range stop butts situated at the east side of the airfield
photo by David Parkin

Drouge towing instruction plate from one of Cark's aircraft
(an identical example was found on the RAF Millom site)

Flare cartridge cap & fuel store key tag

Only surviving building from RAF Cark's 48,000 gallon petrol storage installation (in field, west side of Moor Lane (note blast wall in front of building).

RAF Cark's guard house - now a bus shelter. (Flookburgh end of Moor Lane)

Officers bath house & latrine (west side of Moor Lane)

Station flag pole

Ambulance store and mortuary building situated to left of control tower

rachute store to left of control tower now a stable!

Cark's single Bellman hangar which survives, though now in a worse condition, to the present day.
(photo by David Parkin)

Motor transport building modified but still in use for large vehicles

st shelter with control tower in background
to by David Parkin

Underground battle HQ. Built for Cark's fighter station status situated next to present skydiving clubhouse (note gun slit) Photo by Russell Holden

Officers accommodation block on Willow Lane modified and extended to create a modern bungalow. My thanks to the owners Tony & Mandy for allowing the photos on these pages to be taken on their propert

Air raid shelter made into attractive garden store

Pristine interior of air raid shelter

Double chambered air raid shelter in field at rear of ablution block

Officers ablution block adjacent to accomodation. Greatly reduced in size and now used as a garage

e ablution block has had various uses in the years following the war. At some point a row of clothes
oks ended up in here obviously taken from a WAAF's accomodation block. Sadly only these two
mes (Aircraft Woman Bolton & Aircraft Woman Rowan remain legible enough to photograph. They
me to us down the years as very poignant artifacts.

Brown's houses used as range-staff billet during its use by RAF Cark All photos on this page by David Parkin

Remains of vehicle access bridge to Humphrey Head rifle range.

Wooden support posts for Silverdale bombing range target. Easily visible to passengers passing by train

Concrete access bridge to Silverdale bombing range, now a victim of coastal erosion

Rubble remains of bomb range plotting post onshore near Jenny Brown's point

Section of armoured cable once used to deliver power to bombing target

All official photos taken at RAF Cark during the war years were taken by the Slingsby sisters and processed in their little studio here on Kent's Bank Road, Grange-over-Sands - now an undertakers. Several sets of photographs must have been taken to provide officers and staff with personal copies as over the years from various sources I have been able to gather all but a handful of the 60 staff pilot courses that passed through Cark during the station's life.

I couldn't end this section without showing the airstrip itself still being used today – shown here is the twin engine Brittain Norman 'Islander' owned and operated by NW parachute club, Cark airfield... overleaf is an aerial view of Cark airfield in the 21st Century!

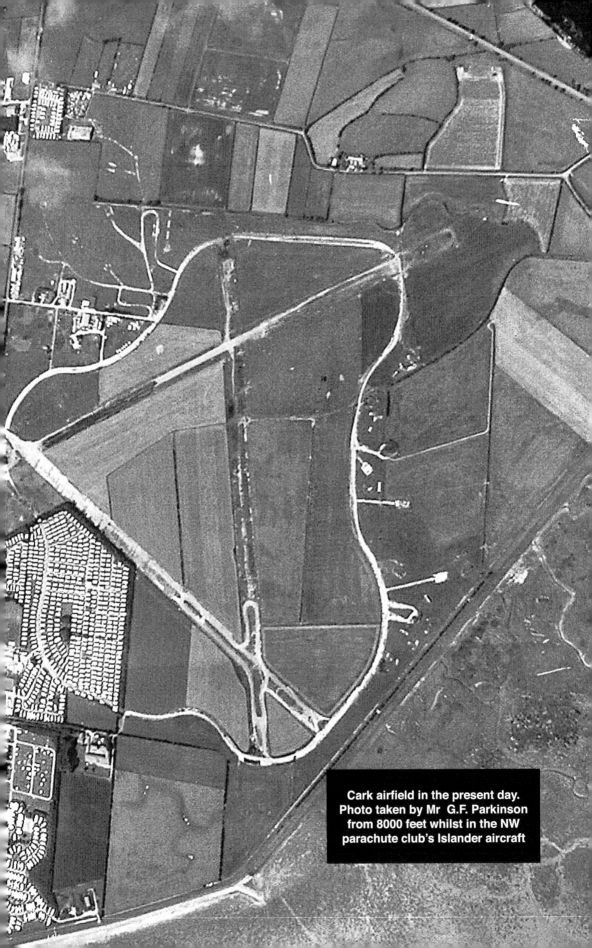

Cark airfield in the present day. Photo taken by Mr G.F. Parkinson from 8000 feet whilst in the NW parachute club's Islander aircraft

CHAPTER 4

RAF Grange-Over-Sands
Equipment Officers Training School

Author's Preface

At the outset of war and with the conflict gathering momentum, it was inevitable that a good deal of reorganisation and redistribution of RAF Training Units would take place. Such was the case with No 1 and No 2 Equipment Officers Schools, who were at that time based at RAF Brise Norton and RAF Little Rissington respectively. In the early summer of 1940 the decision was taken to amalgamate the two units for operational purposes and move the school to a rural northern location.

Photo courtesy of Hotel Management

The location chosen for the housing of the school was the Grand Hotel at Grange-over-Sands and the unit would remain there until March 1944. The purpose of the school rendered service there routine and uneventful for the most part. However in the early days of their stay, the staff at RAF Grange-over-Sands were on occasion involved in very significant historical events as detailed in the following chapter.

RAF Grange-Over-Sands – the formation

The Commanding Officer of RAF Grange was to be Squadron Leader AW Wall. He took up post at the Grand Hotel on the 5th June 1940 having flown in to RAF Squires Gate, Blackpool and completed his journey by staff car. The Officers and pupils of the newly amalgamated schools arrived simultaneously on the 10th June and the unit is recorded as being self-accounting from that date.

RAF Grange's log tells us that problems were encountered with the Hotel's water supply, to the extent that no water was to be consumed before it had been boiled. This state of affairs was to prevail for some time with the unit having to bring in fresh water by Army tanker, though no explanation for the problem is recorded.

The move to Grange appears to have taken place very smoothly. Only two days after the school arrived at the Grand Hotel, training had already begun to complete the courses of the two amalgamated schools. Preparation was also taking place for an imminent new class intake.

High on the list of priorities during the unit's first month in post was station defence, though the school only possessed three Lee Enfield rifles which the unit's log describes as, "On loan from Brise Norton and very elderly!"

On the 19th June it was made clear by Training Command that the station was to be responsible not only for its own defence in the event of an enemy incursion, but also that of the surrounding area. In respect of this, a further 96 rifles and ammunition were delivered to the unit on the 21st June. These were followed by an unspecified number of grenades and two Vickers machine guns on the 11th July.

Don't worry about facing Hitler with only 3 rifles... worry about only having 4 bullets!

RAF Grange's log carries some twelve pages of operational instructions concerning the defence of three strategic locations - Grange gas works bridge, Holy Ghost entrance (Castlehead Lindale) and Thorn Hill - using between fifteen and twenty Pupil Officers with one Staff Officer in command.

R A F GRANGE OVER SANDS
Cumbrian Grand Hotel
Circa 1941 –1944

All the officers in the photograph are Pilot Officers except Flight Lieutenant Smith who could possibly be their Course Officer.

Back Row L-R
G R Wilson, J A W Young, G W Heath, P W Palmer, M R Gould, E L Potter,
S H Pilling, S Walker, W C Wilson.

Middle Row L-R
F H Trott, A E Elliott, G J L Tipping, L A Levoi, F W Brown, A R D Buckle,
D Wishart, J Mumford, W Hollins, W F Youell.

Front Row L-R
J Gardner, W M Woolf, C V F Pavia, H Hesling, Flt Lt G R D Smith, G H Jarrett,
A M Rennie, R C H F Barrett, B Clements.

Using the defence of the gas works bridge as an example, the unit's log records that the defence detachment would be, "One Staff Officer and seventeen Pupil Officers armed with: seventeen rifles with bayonets (fifty rounds of ammunition per man); one Vickers machine gun plus 9,000 rounds of ammunition; twenty-four Molotoff Cocktails and twenty-four hand grenades." Their objective was to present a crossing of the River Winster by the enemy.

It must be remembered that at this time fears of a German invasion were very real and this was being further compounded by the increasing raids on British cities by the Luftwaffe. Clearly Sq/Ldr Wall took the defence of his unit very seriously, for in addition to an armed patrol of the Hotel grounds and a permanent guard on the drive entrance, he positioned an anti-aircraft machine gun post on the roof of the Hotel to be manned at all times.

It is clear that operational defence commitments were putting a strain on staff resources by this point. The station log records a serious shortage of men on the 17th July when asked to provide a guard on a forced landed aircraft out on the sands. The aircraft was a Spitfire piloted by P/O Eugene Tobin who had made a forced landing in low cloud and bad visibility at around 20:30 hours that evening. P/O Tobin was uninjured.

As July progressed the anxious residents of the Furness peninsula became the subjects of regular air raid warnings, all of which proved to be false

Spitfire

alarms. However, on the 19th July two enemy aircraft were reported in the vicinity of Arnside Railway viaduct and an attack on the coastal rail network was thought to be a distinct and imminent possibility.

Perhaps in response to this perceived threat a gun post was established by RAF Grange at Arnside. It was manned by a detachment which was comprised of two machine guns and fourteen Riflemen, with Flt/Lt Hill as its Subordinate Commander. The unit's task presumably, was to protect the rail bridge over the River Kent from attack.

On the 24th July, with their course completed, 120 Pupil Officers received their respective postings and the school received its first intake of Batmen under training. The Batman's duties were as an Officer's Servant and aide so it is fair to assume that ironing was high on the curriculum!

August brought yet another false air-raid alarm, though the month was largely uneventful for the station until around midnight on the 29th/30th of the month when enemy aircraft were heard overhead. Their distinctive engine noise receded as they made their way to Barrow's shipyards. Six high explosive bombs were dropped on Walney that night in what was to be the start of the "Barrow Blitz".

By the time the last German bombs fell on Barrow-in-Furness in 1942, 92 civilians had been killed and 673 injured. The Luftwaffe had dropped 86 high explosive bombs, 34 landmines and 1,300 incendiary devices on the town.

RAF Grange's station log contains little of note for the month of September 1940, though the coming month was to involve the unit in an incident which would become famous the world over and be the source of a book and a film. On the 7th October notification was received from Ulverston's Police Superintendent that a German Officer had escaped from No 1 Prisoner of War Camp, Grizedale Hall and that a search party was required.

For two days the unit helped search the area surrounding the POW Camp before being stood down to return to normal duties. The German Officer was recaptured some five days after his escape. His name was Oberleutnant Franz Von Werra and this is his story...

Franz Von Werra, Fighter Pilot and Escapologist

It has been a subject of debate over the years as to whether or not Von Werra was the "fighter ace" as portrayed in German propaganda at the time, or merely a construct of the same to provide an air hero for the nation. What cannot be called into question however are his determination, courage and resourcefulness in his ultimately successful attempts to escape.

On the 5th September 1940 the Luftwaffe launched a raid on the town of Croydon. The raid was to be a distraction whilst a main force attacked the fighter base of RAF Biggin Hill. The bombers which attacked Croydon on this occasion were being

187

escorted by some thirty Messershmitt 109's, of No 2 Gruppe, third fighter Geschwader. Shortly after leaving Croydon three Spitfires in near vertical dives broke through the German fighter escorts to attack the bombers below whilst firing short 'covering' bursts.

One of these bursts of fire hit the aircraft of Franz Von Werra and badly damaged the Messerschmitt's engine causing a rapid loss of altitude. Realising that a further Spitfire was rapidly closing on him from the rear, Von Werra began a series of defensive corkscrew manoeuvres while the Spitfire continued to fire on him. Faced with the inevitable, Von Werra made a forced landing in a field just east of Winchet Hill, Kent, avoiding injury but being taken prisoner immediately by members of the nearby Searchlight Battery. The time was 10:00 hours and within an hour conflicting versions of how Von Werra was shot down began to circulate, with the man himself adding to the confusion. The Searchlight Anti-Aircraft Battery stationed nearby claimed to have shot him down and were overjoyed to see that his tailfin carried so many victories, they had shot down an ace! – Or had they?

It is now widely accepted that it was in fact Flt/Lt J T Webster of No 41 Squadron based at RAF Hornchurch who downed Von Werra that morning. Indeed his combat report of that action tallies perfectly with the engagement

and subsequent crash of the 109. Flt/Lt Webster was no stranger to intense aerial combat, having distinguished himself in the skies over Dunkirk, after which he was awarded the Distinguished Flying Cross. He had destroyed seven enemy aircraft whilst protecting the allied troops trapped on the beaches there. Sadly, after shooting down Von Werra in the morning, Flt/Lt Webster went into action again in the afternoon and was killed.

Just over a month after his capture and following several attempts at interrogation it was decided that Von Werra should be held prisoner - along with other Nazi Officers who posed an escape risk - at Grizedale Hall in the Lake District. The Hall was situated in the very pretty Satterthwaite Valley, having been built at a cost of £50,000 in 1903 for the millionaire shop owner Harold Brocklebank. Upon his death in 1936 the Forestry Commission took over the Hall and its extensive estate. They remained in control of it until 1940 when the War Office commandeered the forty room mansion for use as a Prisoner of War Camp.

Within a short twelve days following his arrival at Grizedale Hall, Von

Werra had already begun to plan his escape. Every three of four days a group of prisoners would be taken for an exercise walk under armed escort. Sometimes they would turn right at the Hall gates for a moorland walk, or left through Satterthwaite Village where they would be given a rest stop at High Bowkerstead Corner. Here some prisoners would routinely sit on the wall to smoke and chat.

It was whilst sat on this wall that Von Werra astutely realised that there was a blind spot some fifty yards up the road. If he was able to drop over the wall into the field and make his way there, it would put him out of sight of the guards.

Von Werra's plan was put before the hall's escape committee and it was decided that he should be assisted in his attempt. Major Fansela, Senior German Officer, then contrived to have the time for their exercise walk changed from 10:30 hours to 14:00 hours on the pretext that it interfered with educational classes - Their captors fell for it. The change of time was crucial to the success of the escape attempt as Von Werra would have less time to wait for nightfall, making the search for him all the more difficult.

And so, on the afternoon of the 7th October 1940 the prisoners and their guards arrived at their usual rest stop. Von Werra and a couple of his comrades climbed onto the wall and lay nonchalantly smoking whilst their guards were momentarily distracted by a passing grocer's cart from which they purchased fruit. Upon receiving a signal from a comrade, Von Werra rolled silently off the top of the wall and into the field, after which crouching low he made his way to the blind spot some yards further along.

All could have been lost at this point as he was spotted by two women some distance away who began waving their handkerchiefs and shouting in an attempt to attract the attention of the escorting soldiers. Immediately the German prisoners began to shout back and wave at the women until they were herded back together for the march back to Grizedale Hall.

It was not until the prisoners and their escort arrived back at the Hall that Von Werra's escape was noticed. A full scale search was launched using Ulverston Police Station as headquarters and involving the staff and pupils of RAF Grange- over-Sands.

All were fairly confident that Von Werra would be recaptured very quickly but it was three days later on Thursday the 10th October that the first sighting of him was reported. In the late afternoon of that day whilst checking a stone hut used for sheep fodder near Broughton Mills, two farm workers came upon Von Werra sheltering from the rain there! An attempt was made to detain him but he broke free and fled into the dark once more using the night to aid his escape.

The search was now intensified and moved to the Duddon Valley. Finally, on the 12th October and several days after his escape, Von Werra was spotted by a shepherd who alerted his pursuers. Very soon afterwards he was discovered lying on his back in a bog with only his face showing above the surface – the game was up.

Captured at last he was taken to the Travellers Rest Inn where he was given a hot cup of tea before being moved to Ulverston Police Station for questioning.

When returned to Grizedale Hall, Von Werra was given twenty-one days confinement but did not complete this before he was moved to another POW Camp near Swanwich in Derbyshire. Quite incredibly he escaped from there through a tunnel with five other German Officers! Having achieved his freedom yet again he made his way to RAF Hucknall, where he almost escaped completely. He had fooled the personnel into believing that he was a Dutch pilot serving with the RAF and gained access to a Hurricane fighter before he was finally apprehended!

Enough was deemed to be enough and after a spell in solitary confinement back at Swanwich, he and two hundred and fifty other German Officers were placed on a ship bound for a POW Camp in Canada. A plot to take over the ship was aborted, but once in Canada and travelling overland by train, Von Werra threw himself from the train near the United States Border. It is testament to his grit and determination that in sub-zero conditions and suffering frostbite as a result, he amazingly crossed the St Lawrence River into the United States of America.

At this time America was not involved in the War and Von Werra surrendered himself to an American Policeman. Political arguments began between Canada and the United States, during which Von Werra once again escaped with the help of the German Consul, back to Germany via Mexico, Peru, Bolivia and Brazil.

He arrived back in Germany in mid April 1941 and was promoted to the rank of Hauptman, following which he saw action on the Eastern Front before being transferred to Holland on coastal defence duties. On October 25th 1941,

Von Werra whilst serving on the Eastern front

just twelve months after his escape from Grizedale Hall, Von Werra was flying a routine patrol over the Dutch coast in a brand new Messerschmitt when the engine failed and he was seen to crash into the sea. No wreckage was ever found, nor was his body ever recovered - there would be no escape this time. The story of his incredible escapes lives on in the book and the film of the book entitled "The One That Got Away".

By November 1940 the school had settled into an established routine and was now also providing training for Accountant Officers in addition to Equipment Officers and Batmen. The station's log reflects this routine with nothing of import recorded until the 7th February 1941 when all station personnel were assembled and given instruction on how to deal with incendiary bombs. These devices were extremely destructive and dropped in large numbers along with high explosive bombs, starting fires over large areas and being very difficult to extinguish. The method prescribed for dealing with these devices involved a stirrup pump or hose reel and sand to starve the fiercely burning weapon of oxygen.

On the 14th February an intake of twenty Batmen under training arrived at Grange to begin their course. Their recorded civil occupations were varied and included Waiter, Dance Musician and Valets. Among them were the Head Waiter of the Bath Hotel, a Valet from the Houses of Parliament and a Waiter from Claridges! What a stellar line up!

RAF Grange was once more called upon to provide a guard on a crashed aircraft on the 26th February. A Fairy Battle aircraft had crashed close to Grange Golf Links, its pilot P/O M.Marczenko was only slightly injured; his aircraft however was completely wrecked.

I've been called up?!?

The month of March was marked by false air-raid warnings on the 6th and on the 12th of the month. Huge explosions were heard in the direction of Barrow when the Luftwaffe once more attacked the shipyards.

Barrow was to receive a further five raids throughout April. Due to this increased activity the anti-aircraft gun position up on the roof of the Grand Hotel was supplemented by an additional airman to act as observer.

The school's log for the 1st May is one simple line, "Routine all sections".

However, May was to prove far from routine in the extreme.

Fairey Battle

On the 3rd May just before midnight, enemy aircraft were heard over Grange and an attack was anticipated. To everyone's relief however, no marker flares were dropped and the aircraft flew on. Shortly afterwards the sound of explosions and anti-aircraft fire were heard from the direction of Barrow. One of the largest bombing raids the town would suffer was underway.

The following night at 23:50 hours, the station received an air raid warning, following which enemy aircraft were once again heard overhead. At 00:15 hours the first high explosives were dropped on the town of Grange, followed by an intense shower of incendiaries which struck Kents Bank.

From then on the attack intensified and at 00:20 hours the rooftop observer reported that the Kents Bank area appeared to be well alight. By 00:25 hours it was decided to evacuate the hotel building and station personnel were ordered to the air raid shelters, leaving only a fire patrol and the rooftop post in place.

At 01:00 hours Flt/Lt's Waller, Kearon and P/O Ratut led a party of twenty-five Pupil Officers into the town to assist fire fighting personnel with the several houses which were on fire. At 01:45 hours another party was dispatched to deal with a stack of incendiaries which had fallen on the railway tracks opposite the hotel.

Whilst no incendiaries struck the hotel, a single one landed at the foot of the hotel drive. It was swiftly dealt with by 1314861 Air Craftsman 2 Webber who was commended for his action and later further praised for his conduct throughout the raid.

By 02:00 hours it became clear that the bombing had not been confined to Grange alone. In lower Allithwaite a near miss blew the windows out and

Advert for an incendiary fighting device commonly used during the blitz years

'FYREX'
Fights & wins

with water only

A fire-bomb, surrounded by blazing wood-work, extinguished in 39 seconds ! 200 gallons of blazing oil and petrol extinguished in 2½ seconds ! Just two of many authenticated FYREX Victories ! The FYREX four-in-one NOZZLE equips the fire-fighter to deal instantly with every fire-risk. A twist of the wrist gives either the SMOKE-DRIVING CURTAIN, enabling the operator to approach the source of the fire. FINE SPRAY, saving damage to fragile goods, saving the operator from risk in electrical fires. POWERFUL STRAIGHT JET. INSTANT CUT-OFF, saving water-waste and water damage.

SIMPLE, FOOLPROOF, RELIABLE—easily operated. No vital seconds lost in changing jets.

THOUSANDS IN USE by fire-brigades, munition works, etc.

FYREX UNIVERSAL NOZZLE
UNIVERSAL NOZZLE CO.
Brent Crescent, North Circular Road, London, N.W.10
Telephone : WILlesden 3632

DHB

the roofs from several houses. Meanwhile a further team of Pupil Officers were sent to Lindale to deal with a fire at the garage there caused by a stream of stray incendiary bombs. At 03:00 hours it was felt that the raid was decreasing in intensity. But, at approximately 03:15 hours a lone German raider dropped fares over the Grand Hotel. After making one exploratory run past, he returned and released two heavy high-explosive devices which overshot by a good distance and exploded harmlessly up on Hampsfell, between Grange and Cartmel.

Following this final attack, the raid on Grange ceased, though an extensive attack on Barrow could be plainly heard in the distance. The all clear was finally given at 04:30 hours and personnel were recalled from the shelters. It had been an eventful night to say the least and the personnel of RAF Grange had given a good account of themselves in the face of it. In the aftermath of this incident it was recorded that no service personnel were injured and the town only suffered one serious civilian casualty, and on the 8th May the station received a formal letter of thanks from Grange Urban District Council for their assistance during what the council described as "Sunday night's Blitz".

Once the site of a beautiful house belonging to a Colonel Porritt. Gutted by incendiaries during the Grange blitz it was never repaired and was demolished and rebuilt only relatively recently. Now home to the Yewbarrow Lodge retirement home

In early June 1941 the station received its first intake of WAAF personnel who were to be trained in Mess Stewardship. These ladies were to be billeted on Holme Island and a guard was provided for the narrow causeway which connects the Island to the main shore. Whether the guard was there to keep others out or to keep the ladies of the WAAF in, I have been unable to discover!

Private estate of Holme Island and gate lodge used as guard house when WAAFs were billeted here.

On the 1st August 1941 the school's log states, "A new and fully comprehensive local weapon training scheme has been started for the permanent staff of the Equipment Officers' Training School (Officers, NCO's and men) in view of the fact that the general standard was considered to be low at the time when 100% efficiency has been called for. Each member of staff is now receiving at least one hour daily on arms training, irrespective of his trade, from instructors in the following weapons: Rifle Bayonet, Lewis Gun, Vickers Gun, Hand Grenade and in selected cases Revolver." The permanent staff should be divided into ten classes in order not to interfere with routine work of the different departments. Local boards of efficiency will be arranged. Six hours of instruction is to be given on rifle, two hours to bayonet fighting, two hours on hand grenade range, six hours on the Lewis gun, eight hours on the Vickers gun and two hours on revolver.

Throwing area of Hampsfell grenade trench. My partner Philippa with Rosa the terrier showing depth of feature

Dry stone wall at front of trench

Pre-World War 1 rifle range at Humphrey Head used by home guard, RAF Grange & 1SPTU during WWII

Inert grenade dug up in 1998 by Haverigg prison inmates & confiscated by author!!

Area of grenade trench feature... scale shown by Philippa & Rosa

During the War years my father served in the local Home Guard and helped construct a hand grenade throwing range on Hampsfell (see photographs). Though not so easily defined on the ground by now, it presents as a very visible feature from the air. My father told me that on occasion they would share the range with personnel from RAF Grange and RAF Cark who would arrive by lorry via the road which runs up from Grange through Eggerslack Woods.

Another shared training facility for the RAF and Home Guard was the rifle range to the west of Humphrey Head. It had been constructed prior to the outbreak of WWI for the use of the West Lancashire Territorials and was once more back in use. It is also noteworthy that deep under the Grand Hotel Sqn Ldr Wall had a small calibre rifle range constructed in the cellar; the remains of which are there to this day, though access to the facility is denied now due to health and safety.

The 17th August brought news of another escape from Grizedale Hall by two German Officers and a request for the provision of a search team. One hundred Officers set out from RAF Grange. Arriving at Haverthwaite they began a search sweep across the moors at 07:00 hours. Fanning out and moving back towards Grizedale, they arrived at 11:00 hours having found no sign of the escapees. The two Germans were not cast from the same mould as Von Werra however. Recaptured by the Home Guard close to the shores of Coniston Lake at 12:30 hours, they'd had only six and a half hours of freedom.

The rest of August saw the school settle back into its normal routine uninterrupted. This state of affairs prevailed throughout September into October, until on the 17th of the month the unit was witness to a horrific crash close to the hotel.

At around 16:45 hours a Tiger Moth biplane was seen to plunge onto the sands opposite what was then, Grange coal depot and immediately burst into flames. Cpl N.Mercer and A/Cpl R.Bennett rushed to the scene of the crash but were unable to save the two crewmen, F/O Carlton and P/O Millns who were found to have died from burns and multiple injuries.

Later that day a message was received from Ulverston Police Station requesting assistance in patrolling the shoreline from Holme Island to Kents Bank, in the hope of intercepting a landing there by three Dutch internees. They had escaped from the internment camp on the Isle of Man in a stolen boat. A patrol was provided and a vigil kept till dawn when word arrived that the three escapees had made landfall early that morning near Whitehaven and been arrested by an Army patrol.

At 04:30 hours on the 19th October 1941 a further message was received from Ulverston Constabulary, once again asking for a search party following the escape of a German Naval Lieutenant from the POW camp at Grizedate Hall. A search party left RAF Grange at dawn to search the Newby Bridge, Backbarrow and Thwaite Head area. But, the search was called off at 11:30 hours when word was received that the escaped prisoner had been captured by the Home Guard, who subsequently shot him dead when he made a further attempt to escape from their arrest. The German prisoner was submariner Oberleutenant Bernhard Berndt of U-boat U570 and his story and that of his craft is an interesting one.

The capture of German U-boat U570 viic 500 tons and her refit as HMS Graph for the Royal Navy (all photos via Mr P.G. Yuile)

I would like to express my thanks to Mr Peter Yuile for providing me with the photographs and information which have made this part of my book possible.

About U-boat U570

U570 was built by Blohm and Vass in Hamburg in 1941. She sailed on her first war patrol from Norway on the 24th August 1941. Her Commanding Officer was Kapitanleutnant Hans Rahmlow. His first Leutenant was Oberleutnant Zur See Bernhard Berndt and she carried a total crew of forty-three.

The capture of U570

Number 269 Squadron RAF occupied a base at Kaldadarnes in Iceland. They were equipped with Lockheed Hudson aircraft carrying out anti-submarine and convoy patrols from there.

Lockheed Hudson

At 08:40 hours on the 27th August, Hudson 'S' for Sugar took off for a routine patrol. On board were Pilot Sqn Ldr J.H. Thompson,

Navigator F/O W.J.Coleman, WOP/AG Flt/Lt D. Strode and WOP/AG Flt/Sgt F.J. Drake. Their patrol area started fifty miles south of Iceland and upon arrival there Sqn Ldr Thompson took the Hudson down to an altitude of about one hundred feet above the wave tops. At around 10:40 hours U570 surfaced approximately three quarters of a mile in front of the Hudson. Four depth charges were dropped, which perfectly straddled the U-boat's hull causing sufficient damage to prevent the submarine from diving. The

Pilot of S for sugar Sqd/ldr JH Thompson

crew climbed out of the U-boat's conning tower and showed a white flag, making clear their surrender.

Both Sqn Ldr Thompson and F/O Coleman received an immediate award of the Distinguished Flying Cross for their actions in capturing U570. But, their two Wireless Operator Air Gunners received no recognition at all, very strange and very unfair one might say?

The surrender of U570

During the night the submarine was guarded by a series of Catalina aircraft, until at approximately 22:50 hours the first naval presence arrived. This was the converted trawler HM Northern Chief, some twelve hours after the U-boat's surrender. By dawn on the 28th August six naval ships had arrived to secure the area and remove the German crew from their vessel. Following this, though hampered by gales and rough seas, U570 was towed stern first by the Northern Chief to Iceland, arriving there seventy-two hours after her capture.

Because of the damage to her hull, U570 was beached upon her arrival. After her examination by naval engineers (swiftly sent from the United Kingdom), it was decided that after basic repairs were carried out, U570 should be sailed to Barrow-in-Furness shipyards under her own power for assessment and refit.

U570 arrives in Barrow-in-Furness under her own power for assessment and refit - 4th October 1941

A tired looking U570 now moored in Vickers Armstrong shipyard, Barrow-in-Furness being boarded by a British Naval Officer.

U570, now under British Naval control recommissioned as HMS Graph and in pristine condition leaves for the Clyde on 18th February 1942 for further sea trials.
Her new conning tower pennant number now being N46.

In the command of Lt/Commander G.R.Colvin RN DSO DSC, U570 arrived in Barrow on the 4th October 1941, some six weeks after her crew's surrender. First, she was moored in the Cavendish Dock where the torpedoes were removed and handed over to Messrs Vickers Armstrong Co Ltd for a complete inspection. During this process the (pictured) torpedo tube plate was acquired as the German instruction plates were removed and replaced with English translated ones.

Torpedo tube plate U570 - removed during refit

On the 18th February 1942 HMS Graph - as U570 had now become and been commissioned into the Royal Navy - left for the Clyde, the pennant number being N46 in large white letters on her conning tower - we now had a tame hawk! At one time it was rumoured that HMS Graph had sunk another U-boat, U333, but this story was proven to be unfounded.

On arrival of HMS Graph on the Clyde from Barrow, many trials and tests of the German equipment were carried out. The U-boat was used for the training of crews to detect German submarines during anti-submarine patrols. Following which, HMS Graph did many patrols in the Bay of Biscay and off the coast of Norway on the hunt for U-boats.

The remains of U570 (or HMS Graph) lie off the coast of Islay in the Inner Hebrides, where she ran aground following engine problems and whilst under tow in 1944. By now it was extremely difficult to obtain spare parts as the Royal Navy only held one U-boat and so it was decided that HMS Graph should remain where she came to rest.

The crew of U570

The captured crew of U570 were held in southern England where they underwent intensive interrogation before her Commanding Officer Hans Rahmlow was sent to a POW camp in Canada. Her remaining Officers, including first Lt Bernhard Berndt were sent to be held at Grizedale Hall.

The senior German Officer there at that time was Korveltern Kapitan Otto Kretschmer, himself a U-boat ace of some notoriety. Unknown to his captors Kretschmer was sending to and receiving from Germany, information via carefully coded letters.

In national newspapers and the local Barrow Evening Mail, an article appeared showing photographs of the captured U570 being sailed into a "North western port". A copy of one of these papers was obtained by the prisoners at Grizedale and it did not take long for the captured naval Officers to realise that the "Northern western port" was in fact Barrow-in-Furness.

Whilst totally against the Geneva Convention, the senior German Officers at Grizedale held a "court of honour". They charged Berndt, now the scapegoat for the loss of U570, with cowardice for not scuttling the U-boat and allowing it to fall into enemy hands. He was found guilty and ordered to escape, which with their assistance he did. His orders were to proceed to the shipyards at Barrow and destroy U570, the means with which to achieve this end were unspecified.

It was not difficult to escape from Grizedale Hall though it was very hard to cover an escape for long. After only two hours, at 04:30 hours, the alarm was raised and the hunt for Berndt was on. The centre of operations to recapture him was once again Ulverston Police Station, whose personnel were assisted by the Home Guard and a search party from RAF Grange.

The Scottish Forestry worker in Grizedale Forest was also in the local Home Guard and on the lookout for Berndt. Alex Weir, came across the escaped prisoner on a hillside near Satterthwaite. When challenged Berndt stated that he was a Dutch Seaman trying to get to Glasgow to join his ship. Weir told the German that if he accompanied him back to Grizedale Hall he would arrange a lift for him.

Upon hearing this Berndt dashed off. Weir told him to halt or he would fire. Berndt continued to flee but tripped and fell just as Weir fired upon him. Weir had fired at Berndt's legs in order to halt his escape; however, because of the prisoner's stumble the rifle round struck him in the back, killing him.

Berndt was buried in Hawkshead churchyard, the service attended by his fellow POW's. Some ten years after the War his body was removed from the Hawkshead graveyard. Some say that it was taken back to his home town in Germany; others say that he was reburied in the German War Cemetery at Cannock Chase.

Otto Kretschmer, after being sent to a Canadian POW camp, became an Admiral in the post war German Navy. Hans Rahmlow spent the war years in the same Canadian POW camp, after which he returned to live out the rest of his life in his hometown of Freiburg, Germany.

Alex Weir eventually joined the Royal Air Force and lost his life on the 31st March 1945 during a raid on Hamburg with No 405 Squadron. Squadron Leader Thompson was promoted to Wing Commander and died in 1993. Flight Sergeant Douggie Strode was, up until the mid-1990's alive and living in the Blackpool area.

Meanwhile, back at RAF Grange-over-Sands

It seems that billeting of RAF personnel was a serious concern following the bombing of Grange and the damage to several available properties. It is clear also that this was a concern for Grange Council and signs of friction appear in the station's log on the 22nd October 1941when the following entry was made, "Conference on billeting and matters of general welfare in the town, attended by Commanding Officer, Adjutant, Councillor Kennedy, Superintendent Parker and Mr Wright, Civil Evacuation Scheme Billeting Officer. The conference was called at the request of Grange Urban District Council who brought nothing but utter trivialities as agenda. The continued reluctance of the householders of this district to assist in the War effort by meeting military necessities is deplorable!"

In contrast to these problems, the Equipment Officers' School reached the highest number of Officers under training since its move to Grange. At the end of October, Pupil Officers numbered 327 against an establishment of 220. Another noteworthy feature was that the very first WAAF Equipment Officers' Course commenced with an entry of fifteen WAAF Officers, all commissioned from the ranks.

As 1941 drew to a close it was decided to carry out a full station defence exercise and this took place on the 10th December. The unit's log tells us that, "The exercise consisted of an attack by 230 Officers under instruction which was launched from a concentration point near Lindale, on five key strong points that would normally be held by the personnel detailed under the station defence scheme."

While four of these posts held out, an attack made through the woods on the hotel would have caused considerable damage. A full report on this exercise has been forwarded to Headquarters."

By New Year 1942 RAF Grange-over-Sands had settled into an almost entirely academic role and would remain as such for the coming two years. Routine weapons training continued, in the school, on the Humphrey Head rifle range and Hampsfell grenade range. As did defence exercises continue, though with greatly reduced aerial activity by the enemy over the North West, classroom work was allowed to take precedence in a much more relaxed manner.

There are no difficult questions... just those you don't know the answer to

Final days of RAF Grange-over-Sands

Throughout 1942 and 1943 the most common entry in the unit's daily log was, "All sections normal routine". On Christmas day 1943 with no indication that movement of the unit was to be expected, the Staff Officers served Christmas dinner to the airwomen billeted on Holme Island.

Eight weeks later and out of the blue the school received a message by phone informing the Commanding Officer that the unit was to be moved imminently. This message was received on the 28th February 1944 and on the 15th March 1944 the proposed transfer began. The Equipment Officers' Training School took up post at their new home at RAF Stannington on the 20th March, leaving the Grand Hotel to return to civilian life once more.

The End

In the post-war years Wing Commander Gibb and his wife made their home overseas. During a return visit to Flookburgh in the 1970s at a service in Flookburgh parish church to commemorate Cark's wartime service, he presented the original station flag to the community.

It hangs in Flookburgh church to this day

My thanks to those who contributed to this book

First of all to Mr Dave Parkin who kindly shared his research results on the proposed airship factory at Flookburgh and supplied many latter day photographs of the WWII RAF Cark site. Also, to Mr G.Parkinson for providing a veritable trove of memories and anecdotes from his time spent training and whilst serving at 1 SPTU which paint a vivid picture for us of life at RAF Cark. Many thanks are also due to Mr R Blanchard, Mr I Bain, Mr A.Croxall, Mr A.Dudley, Mr F. Ramsay and Mr L.White for their assistance and support whilst gathering first-hand accounts with which to close Chapter 2 of my book.

And to the team

My sincere thanks go to my very patient and diligent typist Alison Smedley, who insists that my handwriting is perfectly legible, (bless her for that!); to Russell Holden, my graphics wizard (and guardian angel); to Michelle Dacre who first began work on my manuscript and got the project rolling and to my long-time friend, Mr Pete 'The Pen' Langley for his most excellent cartoons – Pete, you're a star!

Finally, my thanks go to my partner Philippa who has listened to innumerable reads and re-reads of my book manuscript without a murmur of complaint – though I did notice her 'glazing over' on one or two occasions!

John Nixon 2012

List of useful abbreviations

A.A.C.U...... Anti aircraft Co-operation Unit	O.C.U......... Operational Conversion Unit
A.G.S......... Air Gunnery School	
A.O.S......... Air Observer School	O.T.U. .... Operational Training Unit
A.T.A. .... Air Transport Auxiliary	O.R.B........ Operational Record Book
A.T.C.......... Air Training Corps	O.A.F......... Observer Advanced Flying Un
AC1........... Aircraftman 1st Class	
AC2........... Aircraftman 2nd Class	P/OFFR ..... Pilot Officer
A.O.A.F.U... Air Observer Advanced Flying Unit	P.O.W........ Prisoner of War
2.B.G.S...... No.2 Bombing and Gunnery School	P.R. .... Photographic Reconnaissance
C.O. .... Commanding Officer	
CPL........... Corporal	R.A.F......... Royal Air Force
CPT........... Captain	R.P.A.F...... Royal Polish Air Force
D.F.I. .... Direction Finding Indicator	R.A.A.F. ..... Royal Australian Air Force
D.F.C......... Distinguished Flying Cross	R.C.A.F. ..... Royal Canadian Air Force
D.S.O........ Distinguished Service Order	R.N. .... Royal Navy
E.F.T.S. ...... Elementry Flying Training School	R.N.A.S...... Royal Naval Air Station
E.A.T.P. ...... Empire Air Training Programme	R.F.C......... Royal Flying Corps
E.O.T.S. ..... Equipment Officers Training School	R.V.V.R. ..... Royal Naval Volunteer Reserv
F/OFFR...... Flying Officer	
Flt/Lt.......... Flight Lieutenant	S/SGT........ Staff Sergeant
Flt/Sgt .... Flight Sergeant	SGT........... Sergeant
F.A.A. .... Fleet Air Arm	S.P.T.U....... Staff Pilot Training Unit
FLT/ENG.... Flight Engineer	SQDRN...... Squadron
F.T.S.......... Flying Training School	SQD/LDR... Squadron Leader
G.R.P. .... Group	T.I.............. Target Indicator
H.C.U......... Heavy conversion Unit	U.S.A.F. ..... United States Air Force
H.M.S........ His Majesty's Ship	U.S.A.A.F... United States Army Air Force
I.T.S. .... Initial Training School	V.C............. Victoria Cross
L.A.C......... Leading Aircraftman	V.H.F. .... Very High Frequency
L.A.U......... Light Artilliery Unit	W/OFF ...... Warrant Officer
M.O.D. .... Ministry of Defence	W/T........... Wireless Telegraphy
M.U. .... Maintenance Unit	W/Cdr .... Wing Commander
N.C.O......... Non Commissioned Officer	W.A.A.F ..... Women's Auxiliary Air Force